A Gentleman's Guide To Avoiding Marriage

The Absolutely, Most Compelling Arguments Man Should NEVER Marry.

By

Kali Pinckney

A Gentleman's Guide To Avoiding Marriage:

The Absolutely Most Compelling Arguments A Man Should
NEVER Marry

Copyright © 2010
2nd Edition

Edited by Carrie Constantino
Cover Photo by Kali Pinckney
Cake Topper by TCP Global Corp.
Published by PinCktank Publishing

ISBN 10 - 1453837531
ISBN 13 - 9781453837535

A Product of the United States of America

Foreword

Marriage is tragic but this book explains why marriage sucks for the man and why you, as a man, should NEVER submit to it. I'll try my damndest to explain this to even the stupidest men amongst us. I'll explain why marriage is a trap that you should be cognizant to avoid to the best of your ability.

This is a must-read book for every single man who must decide whether or not to get married. Not only will it help you decide if you actually want to get married, but it will answer some lingering questions and issues that you must understand if you choose to go through this hallowed rite of passage that so many of us attempt and more than half of us fail at.

One cannot merely "study" the marriages of others and be considered an expert. This is because no amount of statistical data can help anyone else understand marriage any better. You can learn what others do, but you cannot learn to be married. I was a busy dating bachelor, and have been married. As a writer, and poet, I have lived a passionate love life with a plethora of women, many of whom, have deceptively strove to snare me into a marriage. I held off for nearly a decade until my foolish heart was pierced by cupid's arrow after a long night of drinking. I am an expert who strives to stop others from making the mistakes I have made.

I hope to give you some information that will help you survive the experience if you are already married, or help to "guide" your decision that perhaps you're not ready for such a life altering "fairy tale" as marriage - if you are single. I'm going to lead the horse (you) to water. You, as the horse must decide to drink the poisoned marriage liquid. Basically I want to give you information in order to help you avoid marriage, or to make an informed decision in the case you're still willing to risk it and get married anyway.

A NOTE FOR THE LADIES

There is no doubt some women are nosey and will seek any possible way to gain the upper hand on the guy they're trying to trap into marriage. They'll even do so by spying on some random book that is not intended for them. So, if you fit the bill, here's a note for you:

Ladies, this book is written for men and at some point, if you read it, you're probably 'gonna be offended by what you read, but you know what? There might be a positive outcome for you. I'd ask you not to be too quick to dismiss what I write as the ramblings of some man who had a bad childhood or was treated badly by girls in high school or some such nonsense; I've had neither. I have actually had quite the opposite experience with most of my close friends being of the female persuasion. I've covertly used my relationships to gather information and might be considered, "an insider" to the feminine cabal.

If you attempt to understand why I'm writing it, you will have a better understanding of what your

4

man thinks about marriage and why he's taking that lovely stroll down the isle of wedded bliss with you. You'll have many roles in marriage. I know you don't like the idea of having a "ROLE", but we all have roles. Girlfriend, Boyfriend, Wife, Husband, Fiancé, Fool, Lover, Caretaker, Pain-in-the-ass, whatever.

Roles shouldn't be considered negative, and one of your female roles, is simply to keep your man happy. You can continue to believe that you don't have to abide by any roles but I'm telling you that if you don't try to keep him happy and/or content, he won't try to keep you happy and/or content either. If you treat him bad, he'll treat you bad. And we all know where that leads.

So just give this book a quick read and only when you're done, determine whether there's any validity. If you find that there is none, I challenge you to pick any section of the book and ask an HONEST guy whether its premise is true or not. Learn the true answers for yourself. But don't waste your time with asking your fiancé or husband because he has a vested interest in not agreeing with many of the assertions within this book. As a rule of thumb; he hides as much from you, as you do from him.[1]

Let's take off on our little journey!

---

[1] And we both know the kinds of secrets you're keeping from your man.

Dedication

*Although I'm NOT one of them[2], This book is dedicated to the bored and lonely married men out there who are suffering the pains of marriage with quiet strength and resolute dignity. '**O Married Man**, You are not alone! ... And oh yea; I'd like to thank my family, mother, God, sons, all the troops in harm's way, and all the little people, yada yada yada!*

*Rest In Peace **Omar Riedman.** Without, you, I would not have had the courage to engage in this project. It was great writing the book with you.*

---

[2] Because, my wife is the Best Ever; and she may be reading this right now!!

Contents

1

An Introduction

> "By all means marry; if you get a good wife, you'll be happy; if you get a bad one, you'll become a philosopher."
>
> Socrates

First Things First

Gentlemen, **NEVER** get caught reading this book in public. It's purely bathroom reading! If you are single and a foxy-looking lady in tiny tight shorts sees you reading this book, it's safe to assume you won't get a chance to see her butt-naked. Women will likely get upset if they get the impression that you as a man, will entertain such an evil topic. And you won't be able to talk your way out of it either. What can you possibly say after getting caught reading this book in a coffee shop? Proclaim that you were "doing a book report?" If the chick believes that, stay away from her ass because, well, she's an idiot!

Now We're Off

This is a timeless story of why you, as a man, should NEVER, EVER contemplate marriage. There are ramifications of allowing yourself to be manipulated into a marriage and I want to help you single guys out there by passing on the wisdom that only an individual with the blessings and experience of a marriage (or two) can offer. This book will help you by explaining why, and how marriage will supremely suck for you. You will receive knowledge that men who've been married 3 times or more can't seem to learn. You'll learn to avoid marriage through knowledge and the understanding of women, and also of marriage itself. As a wise man once noted; "Knowing is half the battle".

I have already been assaulted by a few of the people that have gotten their hands on copies of this book. Some (women) ask me, "why in God's name would you write this book besmirching the sacred entity of marriage"? Others, (men) ask me why I "would allow this information to get into women's hands". Not because it is wrong, but because I'm messing up the status quo for everyone else. I must clearly note that those who have most aggressively queried my intent have been women. But let's get back to the question at hand. Why am I writing this?

Due to my love of people! That's it! Seriously! I am a compassionate man and I want to help other men... to avoid getting married. This is free (If you got the book as a gift) advice from me to you single men. I want **you** to avoid the pitfalls that many-a-married man has made and later regretted. Take the opportunity to learn from the mistakes of others.

Although I'm extremely satisfied that you bought this book, I recognize that others of you were just curious of the subject. It must be noted that I specifically wrote this book for certain, AT RISK groups that need the help the most.

This book is a bit different because where most books are supportive of marriage to the point of being exploitive, this one is not. We want to save men's freedom. Realistically, this is the beginning of the Men's Rights movement. We are happy to help you rebuild the strength you innately carry within your glowing, and warm man-soul.

This book is for men! I am not going to sugar-coat what I have to say here. My promise to you is to be blunt and direct, and that's about it! If you're thinking about marrying, frankly, you *obviously* need to hear it. But remember me later when you disregard my words and end up in a shitty marriage (oh yea, I swear in here sometimes). And just remember that I repeatedly warned you that marriage would suck this bad. I wrote this book for you if you are a:

1. Single Man
2. Bachelor Moving Toward Marriage
3. You are Married or Divorced (and looking for answers)

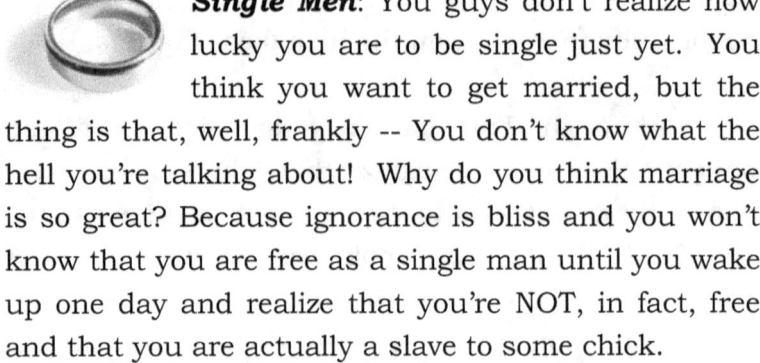 ***Single Men***: You guys don't realize how lucky you are to be single just yet. You think you want to get married, but the thing is that, well, frankly -- You don't know what the hell you're talking about! Why do you think marriage is so great? Because ignorance is bliss and you won't know that you are free as a single man until you wake up one day and realize that you're NOT, in fact, free and that you are actually a slave to some chick.

Alright, I'm sure some of you will take my advice and some of you will not. That's fine! Do what you want; but again, just remember that "I warned you"... and it's not like someone told you in passing. I even took the time to write it down so you can always remember and refer back to what I told you after you've tied the knot and begin to realize how depressed you are!

And now you're thinking about tying the knot? Really? Since you're a guy, it's only fair that I inform you that I know your secret. The secret is that getting married is/was NOT your idea. How do I know that? Because guys are perfectly happy with relationships until external forces begin to manipulate us in to "taking the plunge." You think I'm wrong? Put it like this; any search of bookstores, or your more popular online retailers, will provide any number of titles involving instructions on how women can get their boyfriends to propose to them.

If you didn't know about these books and the virtual industry that's arisen from women (and some douchebag men) trying to instruct desperate women how to "trick" men into proposing to them, you definitely should NOT get married. Some of the more grotesquely named books would include:

- *"Why Hasn't he Proposed"*
- *"His Cold Feet"*
- *"The Get Your Man To Marry You Plan"*
- *"Getting To I Do"*
- *"Closing the Deal"*
- *"Stop Being The String Along"*
- *"The Real Reasons Men Commit"*
- *"Why Men Won't Commit"*
- *"Why Men Marry Some Woman and Not Others"*

And My Personal Favorite

- *"Why Men Marry Bitches"*[3]

Men are truly at a disadvantage in this battle against women who are willing to do what it takes to get married. Single, never married men, should equate marriage to a sports car crashing head-long into a train. They just don't have a chance at coming out unscathed. Women continue to trick man-after-man into marriage but men have to get together and educate themselves and put the same amount of effort into NOT becoming victims of marriage as women put into getting married.

The second group is the **Bachelor moving towards marriage**. You guys are the guys that think you need to grow up and settle down. You think that marriage and a good woman will solve your problems and give you the peace and serenity that your little heart is aching for. You may even want some kids and are so blinded that you're willing to disregard those feelings of concern and doubt in the back of your head for a woman you think you can "grow to love". It looks dumb when you see it in writing doesn't it?

Alright, look, there are plenty of reasons why marriage can be good; but I can't think of any right now! What I'm going to tell you is why you **shouldn't** get married. It largely revolves around the fact that

---

[3] What? You think I would add author information for these books. Go find that information yourself you 'lazy ass.

14

marriage will drag you down and drain you of all of your energy. You will feel trapped, you will feel regret. There's no way around it. Marriage just really sucks!

I stated that guys get married because of external reasons and as an example of these external forces, think of, (1) how your girlfriend is nagging you about getting married. Refer back to (2) your parents bitching about your hell-bound soul because of your living in sin. Another unfortunate external force would include (3) when you knocked that girl up and you thought you had a child on the way only to find she made it all up to get you to marry her. Yep, you know what I'm saying.

Without a doubt, if you're in this group, you're most at risk. The reason is because you're about two drinks away from drunkenly asking your girlfriend to marry you. You should definitely avoid Las Vegas!

Married and Divorced Men: Yep, you guys are also looking for answers. You're wondering why you have feelings of discontent within your marriage. You're wondering why you feel like marriage sucks and you regularly wish you never got married. You wonder why you thought the mere act of locking yourself to some woman would be a good life-idea. You just cannot figure it out; but yet, you have made it your life's work to strive to find an answer to this riddle.

For you formerly married (divorced) guys, you're wondering why the hell you're thinking about doing this again. You understand that madness is repeating failed behavior and expecting a different outcome. Yet, you think that maybe the collapse of your first marriage was because of the crazy woman you married and that it had absolutely nothing to do with you and your jacked up ideas of how marriage is "supposed to be". Just stop short of being a B.B.T., that's a Billy Bob Thornton[4].

Figure out what's wrong with yourself before you attempt to marry again. The truth is likely that your wife may have been crazy; but apparently so is your ass. You actually picked that girl out and married her. It's partially your fault. Accept it, and only then can you move on and hope that you may one day be satisfied with your life.

Listen, you have some serious issues to consider. Marriage should not be a decision one makes lightly and yet, many of us still do it. You must first recognize that "YOU ARE NOT A TRUE INDIVIDUAL"! You are just another guy! Just like all the rest of us simpleton fools.

Your problem is that *you* think you're different! You think you're special! You actually believe that others are making mistakes that you'd never make. The truth is, guys are the same as they were in the 1960's, and even the 1860's. Men have all of the same motivations we did way back when Fred Flintstone was barbecuing Brontosaurus burgers back in the

---

[4] His crazy-ass married (and divorced) 5 times. What an idiot!

16

Stone Age. We want women, wealth, and great (great for us) sex, and that's really about it.

Now, there is the additional group of you that, **know a man getting married**. It is usually composed of guys who are trying to talk a friend out of marriage, or maybe even trying to stop him from heading down the path toward getting married to his psycho chick. Maybe you'll save him from the dreadful error into his blessed union, but hey, even if you can't change his mind - and you won't - at least this book will give him some educational notes on what to expect after he ties the knot.

Many guys begin to think that hey, marriage can't be that bad if you're rational and laid back. What those ignorant guys are suggesting is that they are more rational and laid back than most other men out there and they'll end up different. Despite whether it's true or not, isn't that a bad reason to get married? Plenty of rational people have been married and then moved right into a nasty divorce. Just think of Nelson Mandela, John McCain, or any British Prince, (Even if he was married to Princess Diana).

"Bachelors know more about women than married men; if they didn't they'd be married too."

H.L. Mencken

There are perhaps others of you buying the book for one of your friends as novelty, or as a joke but this is a downright serious subject. Your plan of helping your friend realize he's making a horrible mistake may backfire. Your fiancé-being, douche-bag friend will either thank you for the knowledge and your attempt to help; or maybe he'll try to choke you out. So be very careful attempting to talk some men down from the marriage ledge.

Marriage should be treated just as though you're trying to talk someone out of committing  suicide by jumping off of a bridge and plummeting to their deaths. People have their own reasons for doing it. They've generally made up their minds, and think things will be better afterwards. How can you argue with that? You can only remind them that people who've jumped and survived say they changed their minds after they left the bridge they jumped from. There can be no doubt married men know marriage better than singles.

We all know that some guys will disregard their friends when given a choice between those friends and a chick that he *thinks* he loves... But you should still buy the book for him. And buy an extra one for yourself [in a shameless attempt to sell more books].

2

Why do you want to get married?

> *"Never advise anyone to go to war or to marry."*
>
> *Spanish Proverb*

What Is Marriage?

Here's where I sound conspiratorial; but I do so to help you understand the forces you are standing against. Before you consider **WHY** you want to get married, you have to understand **WHAT** marriage is. Think of marriage as a Venereal Disease. If YOU were to get a crusty, brown-ish, puss-filled, oozing lesion on you junk, a Dr. will have to get past your 2-inch curlies[5], take a swab and figure out what it is before he can give you some medication that'll hopefully make your wiener handsome again. It's the same with marriage. If you use the Scientific Process, you will **only** come up with the fact, you should *NOT* marry.

Well, there is no single, specific, historical origin of marriage. It was most likely of a function of natural law just like in the animal kingdom. Some species tend to pair up with one male and one female[6], while in other species, one male maintains multiple females[7]. What are now western cultures tend towards monogamous relationships, while others lean towards polygamous relationships.

Historically, once the churches gained power, they began to dictate marriage to their followers. Eventually, larger religions became so powerful that they influenced how kingdoms/governments defined marriage. Other cultures continued to accept a man

---

[5] If you actually do have 2-inch pubes, you are thoroughly disgusting.
[6] Geese, Penguins, Christians
[7] Lions, Bulls, Muslims

having multiple wives. Why did the Churches decide to limit marriage? The only possible answer is that it was a function of control.

This control would stem from the ruling point of view. Kings and Governments rule people through the threat of force. Chaos in a country or kingdom is not good for business; business brings in taxes and revenue; revenue requires rules and regulations to collect. People pay for permission (in essence) to get married. The money goes to the Kings and Governments, while those who will marry, must work in order to pay for their lifestyles. If one follows the money, one will find their master. Instead of a whip, thy master uses marriage! Married men *ARE* slaves.

With all of that said, the most likely answer stems from the word marriage itself. "MARIAGE" (with one "R") was a Middle-English word first used in the 14th Century and meant **to match**. In the early days of what we now call "marriage", it was more of a business arrangement and less of a romantic thing. People would trade away their kids (mostly daughters) for animals and grain. Most importantly, no government was involved in these personal affairs.

So to answer the question: Marriage is a "cultural tradition" that varies from location to location. Throughout history, any number of rules have been applied to determine what a marriage is. Sometimes **arranged**; sometimes **polygamist**, and sometimes a **sham**, they always require marriage fees. Why? ***Because marriage is a function of control***!

21

You (or any man) should *NEVER* even contemplate getting married until you can answer the simple questions. I know that requires you to use your brain for more than processing television shows, absorbing football statistics, or remembering which days to take out the trash, but just maybe, thinking rationally might save you from yourself this one time. Maybe, you'll slow down enough to give yourself time to think such a big idea through before you do it.

You must be brutally honest with yourself. Don't pressure yourself into answering immediately because speed is not a factor. Just contemplate your answers for a moment and take a breath and don't glaze over this! Think about it until you have a truthful, cogent answer, and not the generic answers you've been telling your friends and family to garner their support. The question for you to answer is:

Exactly why do you want to get married?

That seems like a simple question right? Well, the truth is elusive and most guys cannot answer the question in a coherent way. Most of us will spit out stupid statements like; **"because I love her"**, or **"we were meant to be together"**. And if that was your answer, go hang yourself right now because that's what you're headed for, an ugly-assed divorce. Seriously! If you ask your buddy and he says that shit, just pimp-slap his stupid ass immediately. This is one of the most important decisions of a man's life and all he can manage is to ignorantly say "love"?

Love, Really?

"Because you love her"? I've got to explain to you the folly of *LOVE*. Love is no answer as to why you should marry someone. **Love is not real**! Love is a figment of imagination. Love is a phantasm. Love cannot be thrown at anyone. It cannot be used to beat someone down. Love cannot be used to refuel your car. Most importantly, love cannot be measured. Why? Simply because *LOVE IS NOT REAL!* One has to **believe** in love because it's just as realistic as a ghost... or a leprechaun.

Everything has something to do with love. There's lovesongs, lovebirds, lovebugs, lovemaking, lovetaps, lovebites, and there's even lovebeads. It's extremely easy to say you "*love*" something. It's so easy that anyone can say they love anything and no one can tell you what love is. Guys "love" their cars! Ironically, many guys will give up a girlfriend before they give up their cars when forced to choose. Does this mean they don't love their girlfriends?

Even **IF** you truly "believe" it is in fact love that makes you want to get married, then you should be able to answer the next logical question. Ask yourself if it is **enough** love? How would you know that you love someone enough to marry them. Is love like a pie? 50% love is enough? Or is love like a power switch? You either love someone or you don't! You must be able to answer that, but alas, you cannot. Why? Because, again, love is NOT real!

If you are using love as your barometer on whether to get married or not, you are going to end up losing half your shit to that stripper you marry in your near-future, drama-filled divorce. Think about it. If you have a dog, you no doubt love it to the point that you'd have to really think about which one you'd rather give up if you had to. Would you rather give up your beloved dog, or give up a girlfriend that you love if she doesn't like your dog? That's what I thought! Love is something you can "choose" to follow, or choose to disregard, again, because it's imaginary. Even if you're on LSD, you can't imagine that something real is not there. Don't let **"love"** dictate your actions. It was a brilliant lady that once noted:

> *"Getting divorced just because you don't love a man is almost as silly as getting married just because you do."*
>
> *Zsa Zsa Gabor*

Obviously, you'd give up the girlfriend because you "love" the dog. Just remember that the moment you get married, your answer gets a bit more complicated. You won't have the ability to simply dump the wife because you will be legally bound to her. Unfortunately, with a divorce, you're gonna lose even more. So your best strategy *if* you get married is to start fights immediately after marriage to see if she breaks. If/when she does snap from your bullshit, go for the quick annulment. Save yourself some time.

To answer the question of "why do you want to get married", a better answer than "love" would include, "because you felt you and your girl might be a good match", or even "because you just want to get married". Why are these realistic answers better than answers with "love" in them? Not only because love is not real, but because these answers recognize that you are getting married because YOU are interested in doing so. Any answer should have **nothing** to do with your lady, other than the fact you're marrying her.

James Brown, always the passionate artist, married three times and had several other long-term relationships leading to numerous kids. Marriage has also gotten him into trouble several times including one in which he led police in a high-speed car chase. Some  of his storied arrests would include assault and suspected abuse of his wives.

Mr. Brown [RIP] would be quoted saying, *"I got a wife who likes expensive things, so she takes all the cash"*. He learned what most women are all about. The lesson you should take-away from JB is that; if the Godfather Of Soul can't maintain his composure around wives, what chance do **YOU** have. You're only the Godfather of some stupid kid!

Either YOU want to get married or YOU don't. No external pressures such as a children-on-the-way, or fathers-with-shotguns, should be a factor to your getting married. It is ironic that women want to hear these dumb, irrelevant statements about love from men, but women practically force men to make these "love" statements when they ask stupid questions like, "Why do you want to marry me"? Utterly Ridiculous!

If you want to know how much of a requirement love is to a marriage, look no further than India. In India, a significant percentage of marriages are "arranged". Love isn't factored in and yet, their rates of divorce are extremely low. "Love" alone is not a good reason to marry.

If there were an internal reason you want to marry, it should be because you realize that living at home by yourself is not fun. As a single man, you'll dream of finding a companion. Dogs and your silly little fish will only work for a short while. Eventually, you'll need conversation and maybe a little bit of naked, sweaty [dare I say perverted] loving. For some fascinating reason, you'll begin to think that dating random chicks and having crazy sex with sluts is hallow. You'll think a wife can provide stability. How wrong you'll be. Don't confuse stability and boredom.

I have commissioned a POLL so that you may gauge your ignorant single-man ideas with married men's actual experience. Hopefully these findings will be insightful and valuable to you. Don't dismiss it too quickly or you'll miss something important.

Marriage Satisfaction Poll Of Married Men 2010**

The following questions were posed to men who were to answer the questions as read. All subjects were to disregard the status of factors such as finances and children and merely asked to focus on wives and marriage.

1) Would you marry again knowing what you know now?
   a. YES --------- 15%
   b. MAYBE -------- 10%
   c. NO ----------- 75%

2) Do you consider yourself "happily married" currently?
   a. YES --------- 5%
   b. MAYBE -------- 10%
   c. NO ----------- 85%

3) Would you be "OK" if you were NOT currently married?
   a. YES --------- 95%
   b. NO ----------- 5%

4) Do you believe any man could be happy within the confines of marriage?
   a. YES ---------- 55%
   b. MAYBE -------- 15%
   c. NO ----------- 30%

5) Do you believe your wife is your "ideal" match?
   a. YES ---------- 15%
   b. MAYBE -------- 15%
   c. NO ----------- 70%

6) Do you consider yourself "Stuck" in marriage? (co-property/pride/finances)
    a. YES ---------- 55%
    b. MAYBE -------- 25%
    c. NO ----------- 20%

7) Could you foresee getting married again in the case you were to ever divorce?
    a. YES ---------- 10%
    b. MAYBE -------- 10%
    c. NO ----------- 80%

8) Have you given up on the romantic ideal of the "perfect" marriage?
    a. YES ---------- 60%
    b. MAYBE -------- 35%
    c. NO ----------- 5%

9) Would you currently recommend marriage to a young guy asking for your advice?
    a. YES ---------- 0%
    b. MAYBE -------- 10%
    c. NO ----------- 90%

10) Do you feel your wife respects you as a man and as a husband?
    d. YES ---------- 0%
    e. MAYBE -------- 25%
    f. NO ----------- 75%

End of poll[8]

---

[8] This zero-blind, non-scientific poll, was taken with a sample size of 20 dudes whom the pollster personally knows, Some of whom are married, others of whom are divorced and remarried. The margin of error can be as much as 47.6 points +/-.

OK, there may be some issues with the poll, but you know what? Those guys answered with their real thoughts and opinions (once I assured them that their answers would not be associated with their names). What can you learn from the poll of married men? That perhaps if so many married men have negative ideals of marriage, and you've never been married, that just maybe you might want to listen to the experience of others.

You have yet to realize and learn that when you become a married man, you will dream about being single again. You can either be unhappy by yourself, or you can be just as unhappy with a spouse. That is your true choice because humans are social creatures by nature. Being alone is never an ideal proposition, however, many guys will realize after being married for a couple of decades that dating random chicks and sleeping with sluts is preferable to being married.

> *"Take my advice buddy, you probably got a 'lotta women pressuring you into marrying them but, don't do it, marriage leads to everything bad in life.."*
>
> *Al Bundy*[9]

---

[9] Married With Children – Fox (Don't act like you didn't watch it).

The Fable Of Jesse The Mouse

For years, Jesse the Mouse was starving and constantly searching for something to eat. Jesse sniffed, sniffed, and sniffed, and smelled every waking hour of every day. He didn't so much feel hungry most of the time as he felt he should always be searching. It was what good mice do! One day he got a whiff of something sensually sweet and his senses went awry. His urge to hunt and eat that tasty morsel of food was so strong he couldn't resist it any longer.

As he got close enough to see the food, it was a sight to behold. It was a shapely and warm chunk of cheese and he realized that this was **too** perfect. In his little head, he thought this had to be a trap, 'but it was so perfect, Jesse ignored all of the red flags and all of the warning signs because he felt that he may never have to search for food again. Jesse moved in and began to put his tongue on that cheese he *thought* was sent from the Gods themselves. He prayed the cheese wasn't moldy since he didn't want to get any warts on his tongue... but this delight was surely worth the risk. Until he heard a loud:

SNAP! "What-The-Fuck"?! Jesse yelped. Next thing Jesse knew, he was waking up in pain, couldn't breathe, wondering what the hell just happened and how he could be in such excruciating agony. Jesse had no idea what the deafening, snapping sound was, nor did he know what the weight that lay on his shoulders was. All he could understand was the throbbing pain. What could it be?

He was married!

Now, obviously, I'm no Aesop[10], but Jesse's Fable should carry some wisdom to you. Jesse The Mouse searched and hunted and starved for a lifetime and when he found his piece of cheese, it was a trap. That is what marriage serves as for millions of men around the world. A deadly trap to be avoided!

Just ask your married friends what it's like to get married. The guys might require a bit of alcohol, but after a couple of drinks they will say something like, "it all happened so fast", or "Dude, I don't even remember getting married"... Just like Jesse the Mouse! If you inquire further about what it feels like to be married, more than 70% will tell you directly that marriage is painful. And there can be no reasonable doubt that, *it is*!

---

[10] Go ahead, go Google him if you graduated after 1994. It's not your fault! The public education system failed you.

Decision to Marry

Just like Jesse the mouse, we all have to make decisions in life. Some of these decisions are not very easy but all decisions have positive or negative impacts on your life. Still, there are plenty of decisions that are made merely because you chose to make a decision. Marriage is one of these, "elective" decisions[11]. Elective marriages, just like the surgeries, are not necessary. Every year, millions of men voluntarily choose to castrate themselves when they don't have to. Why would you risk it?

When it comes to marriage, you need to be mature to make this decision. It is without a doubt one of the most significant decisions of your life. It will affect, not only your happiness, psychology, health, your personal will to live, but also your freedom and perhaps - when you least expect it - the children that will come about "unexpectedly".

> *"Weddings make a lot of people sad.*
> *But if you're not the groom,*
> *It's not so bad."*
>
> *Marlene Dietrich*
> *Make'in Whoopee"*[12]

---

[11] Note that I used "elective" in the same way as one describes elective surgery. I thought it was pretty witty too.

[12] Have you listened to this song lately. This is Marriage in a nutshell.

 There is also another key point you have to understand if you decide to select a woman to marry. You may believe a particular woman is "special". But as you make your decision, understand one thing; **For every guy married to a chick, there's a guy wishing he wasn't married to her**. Some call it the human condition that whatever we have, we want better and that's unfortunately true with relationships and especially with wives.

The Marriadox

Now obviously, arranged marriages would not really work in the US because, well, (1) women have rights and, (2) no American would listen to what a parent says about their personal relationships. Westerners have individual expectations. And because of this, we have what I like to call, the Marriadox; or for some of the more, simple minded of you guys out there, the *Marriage Paradox*. It states that:

"You want to marry someone you know, but you won't know someone until after you marry them." 12

---

[13] When you see a Key, there is information that you should stop and study for a moment.. All of the keys are in the back of the book also.

Yep, you got it. As the Marriadox suggests, you should only marry someone who is an excellent match for you, but the problem is that you likely won't know you are a great match until AFTER you're married. Quite a bummer isn't it? This is a fundamental problem you'll have to acknowledge if you hope to be in any semblance of bearable marriage. We've already discussed the fallacy of love, but you should remember the immortal words of the incomparable Tina Turner; *"What's love got to do with it?"* Nothing! You need to know yourself and know your enemy, and marriage is the enemy of freedom!

Disregard love and search for a realistic barometer. If there were some kind of secret system for figuring out who is our perfect match, the inventor would make billions of dollars from people who understood the real problem. We've all seen those marriages that appear good from the outside but all marriages have their ups and downs. Most are failing.

The more you know about any individual marriage, the more you will realize that there are

plenty of problems in that marriage as well. Problems will become so obvious that you'll wonder how you missed such overt and glaring inconsistencies. This is likely because all married couples will continue to learn evermore about their spouse that they just cannot stand, and dare I say, will come to hate!

Every once in a while, a younger, single guy will ask me what I think about marriage. The conversation always seems to go like this: "Hey Kali", to which I answer, "Hey man, What's up?"

> **Them:** How long have you been married?
> **Me:** 12 years
> **Them:** Are you happy as a married man?
> **Me:** Nope!
> **Them:** Do you still love your wife?
> **Me:** Sure, but what's love got to do with it?
> **Them:** Why did you get married then?
> **Me:** I thought it would be OK.
> **Them:** Would you get married again?
> **Me:** (**Emphatically**) Hell No! Never!
> **Them:** Should I get married?
> **Me:** (**Emphatically**) Hell No! Never!

Millions of married men have had similar questions asked to them by single guys trying to make the right decision for themselves. For many of you -- even though you got this book -- you're still planning to jump off the "cliff of freedom" and happiness into a typical, suck-the-life-outta-you marriage. Why? Because you don't listen! If you were listening, you would recognize that you're not even married yet and you **already** think you're stuck! Imagine how you'll feel after you say, "I Do".

Ironically, you single guys who have never been married before, will not fathom and likely reject the experience given by men who have actually been married. You will do whatever it is that you think you must do. A million married men could tell you not to get married and you will still think that you're going to somehow be different than everyone else.

Marriage pretty much sucks and there is no way around it. There's no way for me to say it any other way. The tragedy is that you'll have to get married before you understand what the hell I'm saying. You are just like the rest of us lowly guys. This is why damn-near all of your married friends are unhappy. And you still think it must be them?

What's funny, is that you actually think that you know your girlfriend (refer to the Marriadox) better than other guys knew their chicks when they got married! Because you're ignorant, you truly believe that your lady is way cooler than other guys' chicks, and you actually believe that YOU are smarter than other guys who got married so your odds of a successful marriage are somehow better than that of other guys (who thought they were smarter than other guys, who thought they were smarter, on-and-on).

You can only understand this concept truly if you get married, but the problem is that you have to get married to discover this answer (again, refer to the Marriadox). But, check this out, maybe the below reference will illuminate the scope of the problem for you a bit. Marriage is based on the principle of being permanent. Yet, after a divorce you will only want to get away to find out that marrying the wrong person is more permanent than you'd ever believed possible.

The Grand Hypocrisy

Marriage is an institution that is based on being permanent. But on this planet, **NOTHING** is permanent. Seasons change, weather changes, people are born, and people die. As we sit here right now, new mountains are being formed by volcanoes and Stonehenge is being ground down by windborne dirt particles. Antarctic water is being frozen into ice, and every (successful) species of life on the planet is being evolved[14], and the species who are not evolving are going extinct. EVERYTHING changes.

The Grand Hypocrisy is that nothing lasts forever, since this is obviously true, how can we also accept that marriages should last forever? How can both be right? Are we *really* willing to accept that a couple should be together until one of them dies? How depressing would that be? Should we accept that even if you are unhappy, you should stay married? Maybe the answer should be recognized that "nothing lasts forever". Not love, and not marriage!

Even marriage vows suggest that you'll be together, "so long as you both shall live", but this would mean that marriage is somehow more important and permanent than life itself. To suggest

---

[14] Yes People, That does mean evolution is real. Don't deny it, and don't complain to me because you don't believe in it.

that the "love" that you and your spouse share is somehow permanent defies all logic. Most humans don't even know what color they want in a car or know what they want for dinner from one day to another.

All of us men that successfully lived to be over the age of 40, can tell you that we were far different people when we were 20, or 30 years old. Another can-o-worms to contemplate is that if we change from year to year, how can our feelings toward another person not change over the same amount of time? The truth is that any concept of the permanency of marriage is some bullshit and we all know it.

If life itself is based on a cycle of creation and destruction and we can accept the premise that nothing can last forever, not even the earth, how can marriages be permanent? Marriage has to be subject to the rules of the environment to which it lives. Its basic physics really. The earth has gravity; therefore, everything on the earth has gravity. The earth has a cycle; therefore everything on earth has a cycle. The earth is going to be destroyed someday by a rogue comet; therefore, everything on the earth will be destroyed. It's pretty simple really!

EVERYTHING (yes I'm over-stressing the fact) has a beginning, middle, and an end. It is not necessarily sad but it is just, *the way of things*. But in recognition of such, this observation reflects the Grand Hypocrisy of Marriage.

One of 1.147 Billion Infamous Marriages

Most people do not know the name, J. Howard Marshall [RIP], however, on the 27th of June 1994, Marshall married the voluptuous and tasty Anna Nicole Smith [RIP]. The couple met at a strip joint where Anna Nicole worked as a stripper. The marriage itself lasted for 13 months until J. Howard Marshall died a content man. Anna Nicole was 26 years old when they married and Marshall was a spritely 89 year old Billionaire.

What can we learn from this marriage? That with the exception of not having a solid will on file, we all should be as lucky as Mr. Marshall. Why was he lucky you ask? Because he didn't marry for some misguided idea of "Love". He married her so he could look cool. There's no doubt he felt alive, virile, and pimp-ish by having a young (but legal/adult) hot fox fondling his old, hairy, sagging balls. She married him for the money, he knew it, and both were content with that arrangement. The truth set them both free.

3

What Marriage is REALLY like

"Marriage changes passion - suddenly you're in bed with a relative."

Author Unknown

Now it's funny that all people – specifically women – bring into marriages any number of ideas they've had since they were kids. Most of their marriage ideas are due to what they saw in fairy tales like Snow White or Cinderella. Obviously, it should be no surprise that marriages don't look so flowery; and no prince is involved.

Marriage Boredom

Marriage is by nature, boring! We call it stability, but it really just means *boring as hell*. Men contemplating marriage don't seem to understand or fathom that they'll have to wake up to that same face every single day unless they're lucky enough to be an airline pilot and fly away twice a week or a soldier and leaves for months at a time. You've heard men talk about how happy they are at the fact they get away from their wives every so often and if you get married, you will be as well!

The saying that, "absence makes the heart grow fonder", is pure bullshit! It suggests that when a man's not right next to his wife that he kind of begins to miss her. Sounds great but in reality, most married guys are just fine when we are left to our own piece! (I mean peace). So whomever says that, "absence makes the heart grow fonder" to you, DO NOT take marriage advice from them! Most likely they've never been married! Also, reach back, use you full balance, and briskly pimp-slap them for me!

Compromise

One thing that few newly married men are prepared for is the requirement for them to slow down and "consult" with another party prior to taking action. We men are hunters! We have the urge to just **go** and **do**. Men are genetically hard-wired and biologically designed to go anywhere in search of things to hunt, kill, and conquer. Just like the United States Air Force, men want to "kill things and blow shit up".

But when you get married, you will be forced to compromise on your goals, dreams, and hopes, just to make some chick happy. Here's an example for you to drive the point home. When a man is single, he has interesting and fun vehicles like musclecars, Jeeps, big-ass trucks, and motorcycles. After he gets married though, he finds that he ends up having to get more "reasonable" vehicles like sedans or minivans.

Wives may not **FORCE** him to get rid of fun vehicles because they understand they can't, but they will set the stage. Smart women, on the other hand, would "FORCE" their husbands to keep their fun cars because smart women understand that their men are happy with those vehicles. Women proudly proclaim, "I didn't make him get rid of it!", despite the fact that they know it was because of them that the husband got rid of his car. Ironically, after the divorce, that man will long for that car back. Don't fall for such primitive shenanigans.

When wives want to compromise it means that they take away something the husband likes and they actually lose nothing. Just think about housing. Guys could live in an apartment[15] happily for years but are forced to buy houses because they're wives "really want one"! The guys will lose out while the wife gets pretty much what she wants. Compromise is a one way street to wives.   You can call this "compromise" if you want, but... few Minivans are fun... exactly like few wives are fun.

Speaking of Cars and Compromise, a friend of mine, Michael[16], explained how his wife wanted him to sell his blue Camaro because it was taking up too much space in the garage next to years of unused and unnecessary crap that finds permanent storage space in garages.. After years of nagging, Michael made a deal with his wife that if she got rid of the 20 years of furniture and junk on the other side of the garage, he would sell his cherished Camaro. They shook hands on it and he sadly, but promptly sold his beloved ride.

To Mike's surprise, his wife first started parking in the spot where his Camaro used to reside, and then, adding salt to the wound in his soul; wifey never sold the random furniture and junk. Damn-near, two decades later (22 years actually), Mike is still kind of annoyed, but he has learned the lesson about compromising with wives. It won't happen again!

---

[15] Ahh, The infamous and beloved Bachelor Pad
[16] Not his real name; but I wanted to steal his story.

This is what compromise is to women and wives. They benefit while the man/husband gets nothing. Currently, Michael is looking for another Camaro. Men should do everything possible to NOT fall for these tricks. Never Compromise! Learn from Michael's mistake.

Yes Dear

YOUR compromise will always, and invariably lead to "yes dear". Once married, you will get to a point where you realize that the only time you hear from your wife is when she wants something from you, or she wants you to do something. When you don't do what she wants, when she wants it, she'll turn into a flaming bitch. She'll complain and be passive-aggressive and talk about you to her sister and mother. She'll make your life suck more, all because you don't want to do what she wants you to do.

Based on this, you will realize that you are in a no-win situation. You will be considered (1) a lazy asshole if you don't do what your wife wants, and you become (2) a slave if you do what she wants all of the time. This will piss you off and you'll never get used to it. Eventually, you'll strangle her in her sleep![17]

The defense that many men begin to take is the "Yes Dear Syndrome". Many married men just give up and say they'll do whatever[18] so they don't have to

---

[17] I should'nt have to say this, but: Don't actually strangle your wife.
[18] Men, try not to actually say "Yes Dear", that just sounds stupid. And everyone knows you're being condescending.

hear any complaints from their wives. Even the biggest, baddest biker dude will get to a point where his "old lady" will force him to decide what is worth fighting for and what is not. All men just eventually give up and say "whatever". All because they want peace! No man wants to fight so they just do whatever helps them avoid conflict at home. And I contend that the yes dear mentality is no fun either.

Although wives may get what they want, they *should* treat this as an insult. It means that their husbands don't particularly want to hear from their wives, and that they don't even care enough to fight them anymore. It also tells a woman that her husband or boyfriend is deep in the process of NOT taking her seriously. That she is becoming a bore and that if he had a way out, he would take it and run.

Marriage is difficult. Too many of my married friends come to me with the problems and issues they are dealing with within their marriages. Do I care? Nope! But it is hilarious to hear about the relationships of others. It's also quite therapeutic trying to fathom the issues in relationships... Other than in my own little, "slice of heaven" marriage.

Have you ever had a girlfriend that just talked too much and really just pissed you off until you had no choice but to dump her crazy ass? Yea, me too! Now imagine a wife that just can't seem to shut the hell up! Imagine being forced to live with someone who seemingly loves to bust your balls. The difference between a girlfriend and the wife is that you won't be able to kick your wife out of the house because some stupid Judge will get to you and make you pay.

Marriage is so difficult and challenging that even the honorable Nelson Mandela was forced into getting a divorce. Mandela was jailed in South Africa by its racist apartheid wielding government for his 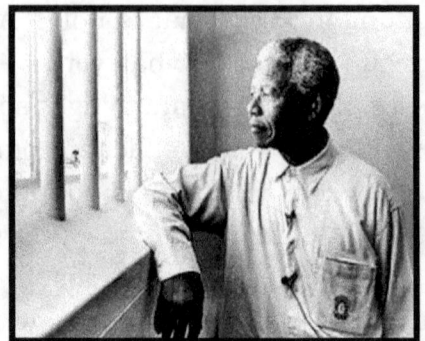 hideous dream that all South Africans could be equal! – *The Horror, The Horror*! Mandela was sometimes physically abused, and other times he was mentally abused. His captors kept in solitary confinement much of the time knowing it was sometimes more devastating to a human than even most beatings.

After being released from prison, he went into a separation from his wife after finding out she cheated on him while he was locked up during his 27 years in confinement. He described himself as, "the loneliest man", and noted that his wife would not even enter their bedroom while he was awake. Ouch! Mandela's divorce shows that despite how amazing of a man you may be[19], or how much turmoil you can withstand, marriage is difficult. If Nelson Mandela can't survive a marriage[20], what chance do you have?

---

[19] Or think you may be.
[20] Nelson Mandela has been married 3 times, has 2 divorces. His current marriage was politically negotiated at age 80.

Another Unfortunate Tale Of Marriage

I was talking to my cell phone guy one day in the mall and he was telling me of his unfortunate marriage. He married his high school sweetheart after reconnecting with her after college. They dated for a few years and he watched her transform from a cool, stylish, sexy, young lady into her current bitch form.

His mother didn't like the girl; his friends didn't like her either. He even got to the point that he didn't even tell his best friend that he got married until 5 months afterwards. After tying the knot, they eventually had a kid (presumably his) and quickly they had a second (presumably his) child. The day we talked, his oldest kid was 4 years old, and his wife hadn't worked in 5 years despite their agreement she was going to pursue her career.

She plumped-up (got all fat) and stayed that way and is now self-conscious about her weight to the point he cannot hang out with his friends. He told me of a instance he had to turn down a Lakers basketball ticket he was given by a co-worker because there were going to be women there... Yes, there! There were going to be women AT THE STADIUM! If she couldn't go, he couldn't go either. Damn! I stood in quiet awe listening and quickly realized I wouldn't have lasted in that marriage.

He is unhappy, wants to leave, but won't leave his children. He has no control and feels trapped!

Yes Gentlemen. This is what marriage is really like. It is patently obvious what's going to happen. And even knowing this, you do not want to believe it. You are going to disregard everything I say concerning marriage and still jump off the "cliff of freedom and happiness" into a life of nuptial hell. Why?

Because no one can tell you a damn thing and if they did, you wouldn't believe them anyway. You believe that since it's you and (...you're so smart) you'll be different than everyone else, and that's OK. But you're not the first guy to fall for the marriage trap, and obviously you won't be the last. You're just more stupid, because you're still going to do it and you have access to the information in this book.

A central problem with wives is the same as the problem with women in general. If a guy said the same things to other guys that women/wives say to their men, they would get their ass' beat. CHECK IT OUT! If a guy walked up to you and called you a lazy, fat-ass, that has a small dick, that guy would understand why he's taking a punch to the pumpkin. But when a woman says the same things to her husband, the guy is supposed to just accept it?!

Now, I in *NO WAY* think that spousal abuse is funny or a joke[21]. But with that said, it seems that women should recognize that some of the things they do are just about torturous to men. No one likes to be teased... not even us lazy, barely-endowed, simple

---

[21] ...except when a husband has Battered Wife Syndrome.. That shit's funny!

men. All we ask is that people treat us like the adult-males we pose as.

But guys should understand that when you get married, you will end up seriously disliking the person you marry. It happens to everyone. You will fall out of love and maybe - given enough time - a spark will come back, but maybe it won't. As we discussed, nothing is constant and nothing lasts forever. That's the truth! Your marriage goal should be to extend your happiness in marriage and hope it lasts longer than the average. It is merely a function of marriage that must be dealt with... and yes, it will suck balls!

... But hey, it'll be OK, you'll learn that you can just self-medicate with alcohol, yard work, or internet pornography every time you start feeling down and blue; just like every other married man you know.

The Marriage Institution

> "Marriage is a great institution, but I'm not ready for an institution."
>
> Mae West

You've heard married people, maybe even your parents, say hundreds of times that they feel "trapped" in their marriages. Why would so many people say this if there was no value in it? Because it's true and after about a year in, many feel stuck.

After 4 years we begin to feel trapped. After 7 years you're itching to escape[22]. Once you get married it takes so much effort to get out of it. You'll be like a Brontosaurus slowly sinking in a Tar Pit.

If your girlfriend is NOT as afraid of marriage as you are; DO NOT marry her!

Why is this? Because your girl has some-how and some-where learned that marriage is "***natural***" and "***just something girls do***". Either you're rich and she has nothing to lose, or she's carrying another man's baby and you'll find out the kid's not yours when you're getting a divorce. Even women should be nervous of getting married. Especially to your ass!

For most people, it is inconceivable as to why marriages fail at the rate they do. It seems ironic that in the places with the most freedom, you have the highest incidence of divorce. True that in free cultures, choice is there, while in poorer countries, cultures tend to look at women as less free[23]. Let's look at marriage itself.

We've discussed numerous reasons that marriages fail and there are several themes that continually recur in all of these reasons. These are Communication and Male Guilt.

---

[22] *The Seven Year Itch.* Marilyn Monroe. Oh, now I get it!!!
[23] Religious, cultural, lack of female civil rights.

50

We've all heard it before. Communication is required in all marriages. I can accept this, but communication can NOT really be the problem. If it were, how would one explain why many cultures throughout the world, and even subcultures within the United States, not seem to be laden with these "Communications problems" despite their poor educations and lack of modern interpersonal communications. The real problem must be cultural.

In our western culture, both people in a couple have to be *synched*. We all recognize that marriages-by-phone don't work. This is why Hollywood couples break up so quickly. You cannot have a relationship with so little communication and expect it to be strong. Virtual presences do not work. But the sad truth is; I don't know one marriage that does not have these same communications issues.

Of the more unfortunate side effects of marriage are the guilty feelings the man will be forced to live with. Now, no one told me about this before I was married but I think you should know about it. Not only will you have feelings of guilt for NOT doing as much as your wife does, you'll have to live with her incessant bitching and whining about it. But despite it all, your wife will never understand that you're not wired the same way as she is.

Women are primary childcare givers (as well as the 'birthers) and women will do everything they can to remind you of it. You'll feel guilt for everything you do, or don't do. You can't win! There are a few classes of man-guilt, two of which include:

1. Doing things she doesn't want you to do
2. Not doing things she wants done

You'll find that there is really nothing you can do to minimize the guilt either. It is not uncommon to meet a guy like Jake:

Jake has been married to Alicia (Ally) for seven years. Due to her poor attitude, selfish behavior, unrealistic expectations, and constant harassment, Jake is extremely unhappy! Jake and Ally have no children and he has realized he and his wife have little in common. His guilt betrays him. He feels, that he has put her into a position in which she has no power. He doesn't want to hurt her because he does truly "love" her. But Jake wants out and he wants out now.

But he won't leave because he asked her to marry him and then he promptly took a job and moved her away from everything she knew. She doesn't make enough money to survive without him and she has no real education. He doesn't want her life to be worse after he leaves. His male guilt will not allow him to "just" leave. Where would she go? How would she survive? It just "wouldn't be right". Jake has learned how aggressive guilt can be and he is willing to be unhappy... for a while!

He's making a common male mistake and will realize it only after he becomes truly marriage-stuck[24].

---

[24] children, grown-up career, life insurance, savings plans, favorite auto mechanic, mortgage payment. He'll lose half in a future divorce.

Your Married Sexlife

> "As to marriage or celibacy, let a man take which course he will, he will be sure to repent."
>
> Socrates

Do you know why there are so many jokes from married men about how sex stopped when they got married?

Because its true! Sex is one of those issues that will most likely tear your marriage apart. Not only will sex, or the lack thereof, make you wish you could go back to the way things were when you first met, but bad, half-assed, and lazy sex will make you wish you never got married at all.

Now, it's pretty likely that you, as the man, love sex at a level to which few women can really appreciate. Ever since you were 12 years old, you knew there was something about girls and you knew that you had to HAVE them. Now, you didn't know what that meant back then, but now as a dirty old man, you surely do!

Sex compatibility quiz

Take the quiz below. And be honest because no one is watching. There is no scoring to it, but this quiz is just to give you an idea of items single dudes need to be cognizant of and the reasons you need to be worried about them.

1. Is she the best you've ever had?
Yes ◯   No ◯

2. Is she willing to try new things?
Yes ◯   No ◯

3. Does she take charge?
Yes ◯   No ◯

4. Does she initiate sex?
Yes ◯   No ◯

5. Is she willing to discuss sex?
Yes ◯   No ◯

6. Is she a flirt in public?
Yes ◯   No ◯

7. Do you like non-standard sex?
Yes ◯   No ◯

Now, these are basic questions. If you're hesitating with these answers, you may have a huge problem on the horizon. Very rarely do people's sexual attitudes and proclivities change over the course of their lives. The reason this seems to be so, is that an individual's sexual "personality" is based on their individual personality.

If a person is sexy, they are likely sexy in bed. If they are boring or crazy, they are usually boring or crazy in bed. The main point that you should take away from this is that, you likely won't get "more compatible" if you don't start off compatible, you'll just get more bored. As your sex life gets evermore boring, you're done for and you are likely to be on BMT, or Borrowed Marriage Time.

Review your answers below to learn why these questions are important. Maybe you'll get a vibe of why or why you shouldn't marry this "woman-of-your dreams". Take heed and avoid the tendency to disregard the answers immediately. Think of your responses as you review the answer key.

Delete Your Answers - *You don't want your chick to see what you wrote about her in this last section.*

What Does It All Mean??

1. Is she the best you've ever had?

The woman you're thinking about marrying had better well be "one of the best" **humps** you ever had[25]; Why? Because if that's not the case, you will be, at first, reminiscing of your past liaisons, and then you will realize that you must go back and try to get some more exciting sex from somewhere else. It will become a slippery slope for you and a constant battle not to Clintonesque stray episode!

You will already be fighting the urge to meet some "strange" (as in, a stranger), but a boring sex home-front will likely be enough to push you over the edge... And right in the arms of some cheap hooker or worse; some expensive slut. You owe it to yourself and any woman you marry to have done your due diligence to learn as much about sex as you can before you settle. You should know what you like. And the only way to know what you like is to gain some experience from as many chicks as you can **before** you get married and ensure compatibility.

As an example, my memories regularly jump back to those threesomes I had in college or those Vegas liaisons I had when I was young with those rich, older, convention going Cougars (how hot was that?). But I digress!!! You must recognize that as long as

---

[25] ...or at least up there near the top of your list

you stay with her, you'll never forget those "good times", and your chicky should have a natural urge or talent to keep you interested and coming back for more. It is your responsibility to slut around before marriage – *safely of course.*

2. *Is she willing to try new things?*

Obviously, it gets a tad boring sleeping with the same person... for the rest of your life! You are eventually going to have to (1) try new things, (2) expand your horizons, or (3) just give up on sex. I guess you could (4) cheat, but that's risky and probably immoral **if you care about that**. Oh yea, and it's probably also a sin... **if you care about that**.

Now, what most hard-up husbands do is try to push their wives to try new things, but there inevitably comes a point at which he just gives up because she just doesn't really care that much about new exciting sex. Now, if she's willing to try new things, throw new ideas at her and enjoy. You've got to know how lucky of a man you are. You guys may survive as a couple.

Most married guys know within the first few months of marriage what things they'll never be able to do (with their wives). So if you like doing something and your soon-to-be wife does not[26], you'll either have to go crazy in the knowledge your weird fetish is never

---

[26] ...and you cannot get her to drink enough

going to happen, or you'll have to keep trying in the hopes she'll change her mind - which wives don't do! Sorry, but you are royally screwed, so to speak.

If this chick is the type to try anything once and you don't need her to be drunk or high to do it, you'll love her forever. She's wild and likely to be a firecracker in bed, but... the unfortunate thing is, that if she's wild normally, you'll love her but she's probably a bit crazy elsewhere in her life! Good in bed; but she may be inclined to smoke crack! Watch out for this one and enjoy her while you can.

3. *Does she take charge?*

Guys always love a take charge kind of woman. Women who take charge are the ones that know what they want in life. Guys flock to women like this because they require less effort. In the bed and despite our best attempts, women's bodies are a mystery to most men (not me though). So if you have a woman that is willing to take charge and tell her man what to do, all the better.

Men have to be prepared to NOT get sexually assaulted and just accept that it is all too normal for married men to feel sexually neglected. So when you're picking a wife, take extreme care to find a woman who takes charge. If you do not, I assure you that you will meet a take charge woman after you get married and you'll be "puppy-smitten"... And how awkward will that be when your wife follows you and your mistress over to that cheap hotel in Chinatown.

Be careful that you don't confuse "a take charge kind of woman" with a "bossy woman". Where bossy women are the big-fat women that abuse their boyfriends on the TV show *Cops*, "Take-Charge" women are still sexy but they understand that it is not their job to TELL everyone else (especially their men) what to do. No man likes a bossy bitch -- in life or under the covers. But we all like take charge kind of women who know what they want, and how to get it in a sexy, non-ball-busting way... Which usually means they give, you get, and then you do whatever they want. Win-Win!

As a note from personal experience, this is again, one of those personality traits that can't be learned. If someone is not aggressive when you marry them, it's likely they won't ever be aggressive. So CHOOSE WISELY!

4. Does she initiate sex?

If your lady is NOT the, Initiate-sex-when-she-wants-it, type of woman, you're probably 'gonna get bored in the thought that you'll have to initiate sex every time you have it. In fact, it'll get absolutely aggravating merely knowing that you'll have to initiate sex again and again and again... Eventually, you'll just feel like you are begging for sex and then you'll give up on her. Women NEVER seem to understand this and they don't recognize that this is not sexy to men. It's actually very, "*limpening*!"

This is a big thing for us guys. It is extremely confusing because **girlfriends** who do not initiate sex are kind of a challenge for the man to deal with, but **wives** who do not initiate sex are extremely frustrating for the relationship. Now, for the girlfriends, we'll get bored of them and 'kick them to the curb. For wives, on the other hand, you're legally stuck with them. And it's your fault because you failed to choose wisely.

But wives who don't initiate sex are basically letting their husbands know that they don't find them attractive enough to "want" them. Women can deny it all they want but men are animalistic and willing to make it happen whenever the opportunity *arises*. Men fantasize about sexually aggressive chicks. They are real women, and men *understand* this animal-like response, but if wives CHOOSE not to show interest, the man will get annoyed with his own sexuality.

There can be no doubt it's pleasant to know that you have a woman whom you drive crazy enough that she is willing to let you know about it by sexually molesting you. That's good for the male ego. And not many women are cool enough to recognize that it makes us men feel like the manly men we purport to be. Women who do recognize this are special and deserve what they get. That'll be all of your love'in! These women are porn stars in their own minds. 'And men love hot porn stars, whether they admit it or not.

They say that men get married and then get fat; but it's not "being married" that makes husbands fat. It's the acceptance that they are just fat, old, boring, non-sexy dudes, whose wives don't find them attractive anymore. It's the nature of things that dudes get old, but women should do all they can NOT to foster this feeling in their men. Initiate some sex!!!

5. *Is she willing to discuss sex?*

If you are planning to marry a girl who is not even willing to discuss sex with you or a small group of friends, you are asking for big-time trouble. This is the type of woman who will have a child and forget all about the needs of her man. Don't be a fool! This is an example of a woman searching for her childhood dreams. She wants the house, she wants her husband to support her, and she wants kids. When she gets those things, the husband jumps to the bottom of priorities list. All the husband will receive is complete frustration with marriage.

You should feel comfortable talking with her about what you like and what she likes in the sack. It may or may not be a long marriage and if you, as a couple cannot discuss sex before marriage than you're already likely doomed to divorce. It is your responsibility to press the conversation forward. Don't let her off the hook about answering questions. You will suffer your entire marriage if you cannot figure out what your lady likes before you get married.

The crux of the problem is that sex will become an abject afterthought. She may not even want the man she married, or sex may not be all that important to her. You have to ask yourself, is she really that interested in sex itself? To determine if your girl is

61

this kind of woman, just keep asking her questions about sex and try to get her to talk about what she likes about sex. If she is the prudish type, you'll find that she can't answer any of your questions, especially if she's not even comfortable talking about her past sexual experiences.

And you're about to marry her?!?! Ouch! Good luck with that. You will end up unsatisfied and again, probably divorced. The worst part is that you know there's a problem already but you're not taking action to address your concerns. You know how slow you are when it comes to figuring out what women want, so don't marry a woman who has a hang-up with even discussion of sex amongst friends. I implore you to NOT make this silly mistake.

6. *Is she a flirt in public?*

Alright, this is kind of touchy for you self-conscious men with small penii[27], but just ponder it for a second. There is a difference between being a flirt, and flirting with the goal to have a relationship with someone. When your girl flirts and you're right next to her (say to get free drinks), that's cool, that's not what you need to worry about. What it likely means is that she's got a healthy sexuality most men can appreciate. She understands how to treat a man. Don't get jealous over this. She's with you!

---

[27] I think that's how you write the multiple of Penis! Sounds smart though!

Obviously, you find/found her attractive for some reason and her flirty personality is likely one of those factors that interested you. You likely think she's damned good in the sack. Again, this is because she's got that sexuality that a man loves. She flirts with the waiter, with the cops, and that's why you have a blast when you guys go out on the town. She knows how to get what she wants from men and that's why you love her. Getting free drinks at bars and getting out of speeding tickets is always a good thing.

As long as you're confident that she's not sleeping around behind your back (with guys). Congrats, you are one lucky man. I would venture to say that if your chick does NOT know how to flirt, you are already bored with her sexually and you hate going out to parties and social events with her. Sorry, but you know it's true! Choose wisely on non-flirty women because you'll be stuck with her boring ass for a really long time!

If there is a positive side to a chick that doesn't flirt publicly, it's that she is likely so boring that she will never cheat on you or give you any good reason to divorce her. You'll dream that you catch her with the pool guy or mailman so you can divorce her, but you won't. Eventually, you'll just have to be the bad guy and divorce her while random people-you-know accuse you of going through a mid-life crisis.

The best part of a "public flirt chick" is that she's the type that will **let the twins out** during Mardi Gras – for some beads. How cool is that? She's too good for you! And she might bring a girl home for you.

7. Do you like different types of sex?

Without a doubt, you and your chick must be into the same types of sexual fun. If she likes it missionary, and you – as a dude - like to be spanked [whilst wearing cheerleader outfits], it's probably not gonna work out for you guys. Comedian Chris Rock once noted that, "two crack-heads can stay together forever". What he means by this is that if two people share a few most basic fundamentals in common, they can survive as a couple. Sex is one of those fundamental areas. So if you like being whipped and your chick is a Zoro-mask-wearing, black-leather, rope-knot tying dominatrix, you're a match made in S&M[28] heaven. Obviously, it sounds funny but, it is no doubt true.

Sex is so important to a couple that even if a dude is a white supremacist, he can justify having a black girlfriend if she's that good in bed[29]. A man will disregard his friends and even his racist family if he meets a girl that is sexually explosive with him!

---

[28] Sadomasochism; Yes there is a name for the freaky stuff you like; you pervert!

[29] Seriously, that's totally happened before. Before Eva, Hitler dabbled with a black mistress in Regensburg. I heard that in a Bavarian bar once.

Now, you know you're going to need a wild girl if you like varying degrees of interesting and perverted hanky-panky, but not all women will be able to hang with this. You'll need to hold off until you can find the right lady **FOR YOU**. Ask yourself: does she have a drug-laced background? If she has a history of getting hammered or high, you'll absolutely love her. She's a wild-child and likely to be a firecracker in bed, but be cognizant that if she's wild, she's probably a bit schizophrenic too.

It's kind of a package deal! Hot sex equals crazy chick. The key is to ensure this girl has outgrown this stage of her life is time. With age, most wild girls settle down and recognize the risk of their behavior. Go ahead and live with her for about 12 years before you even think about marriage. And you should definitely stay away from Vegas.

What Does It All Mean?

Now that you've reviewed the questions, you have some serious concepts to think about and pay attention to. These questions and your answers should give you some clarity into the sexual issues you will face in a marriage. You also have some real characteristics you can search for when dating. You know who to avoid and you know why to avoid them. If you ignore your answers and marry a chick not compatible with yourself, I hope you think of me every time you dream of what your life **COULD** have been.

And <u>REMEMBER</u>: If you wrote some notes out, make sure you burn, soak, shred, or eat whatever you just wrote your answers down on. Don't come complaining to me when your newlywed wife is asking for an annulment because she found the notes your dumb-ass wrote in this book as you guys were moving in to your new yuppie apartment downtown. We've all seen those episodes of Ally Mcbeal, Melrose Place, or Friends[30], where some nosey ass finds the note that wasn't intended for them to see. Don't let your wife see this. If you answer honestly and your spouse sees it, you will only cause problems for yourself. Don't be that guy!

Since you've taken the Sex Compatibility quiz and got some new perspective. Here's a bit more priceless advice:

Do NOT Abstain Until You Get Married!

This is a huge red flag that there will be issues. It may be honorable to be abstinent (for some) but just remember this! If she's trying to wait until you guys are married (God knows it's not the guy trying to wait), she is probably horrible in bed. If you've never slept with anyone else, you guys are on a collision course to disappointment. Why risk it? Have you ever bought a car without test driving it first? It always turns out bad![31] I'm trying to help your ass out!

---

[30] I've never seen these shows. I swear!
[31] Damn you Ebay

Obviously those traditionally (by which I mean religiously) inclined would disagree with me, but as a modern man, I accept that we are different. But the fact is that you need to have sex with your perspective chick-a-dee! Don't get all offended, just listen to why. Here's my advice:

The Abstinence strategy only works if you're both virgins.

You can think you're going to wait until you're married before you have sex, great, but this only works under the condition that you are both virgins. Just tell her "I" told you that you need to try out the goods before you decide to buy. I'll be the bad guy! If you don't try before you buy... If you don't, you'll be stuck with what you get. Don't be a raging idiot.

If you're both virgins (which is rare, I know), the only thing working in your favor is the fact that **ignorance is bliss!** Neither one of you knows what you're missing, or how bad you or your partner will actually be in the sack. Don't fool yourself into thinking you'll figure it out. Think back to how many times you've heard an old woman say she hadn't had an orgasm until 10, 20, 60 years into her marriage, or even until after she got a divorce and slept with another man. This will be you!

This happens all the time. I know it's not ALL your fault as the guy, but if you're about to get married, go find yourself some hoochies, sluts, or hookers and get some practice *FOR THE LOVE OF BUDDHA*. This book also serves as written permission for you to "safely" get some! You have a responsibility to NOT be ignorant and it is always unforgivable to suck in bed. Just ask your ex-girlfriends (or whoever).

If you're still intent on attempting the "abstinence experiment", you must be able to recognize how it will hurt you. In a marriage, you want to do everything you can to NOT suck in bed. If you do suck, your chick won't want to sleep with you (any more than she does now). When you figure out why your lady doesn't want to sleep with you, your feelings will be hurt at a level that will crush your manly spirit; you won't be able to recover and this will lead you into a death spiral. The less sex you get, the more your eyes will inevitably stray. The more your eyes stray, the greater your odds of taking the opportunity to get some when the opportunity arises.

NEVER attempt this abstinence strategy if your prospective chick considers herself, a "Born Again Virgin". What she's really telling you is that she used to be a slut, everyone found out, and then she tried to do damage control by going to church. If it means anything to you, she's probably still a slut!

No Good Can Come From This!

4

The Five Wife Truths[32]

> *"A spouse is someone who'll stand by you through all the trouble you wouldn't have had if you'd stayed single."*
>
> *Author Unknown*

---

[32] Look here, this is Page 69!

Every man should learn prior to entering a marriage that when it comes to wives, there are five truths that every guy must recognize and accept if he dreams to be happy in a marriage. He must also learn that if he cannot follow these simple rules, he definitely does not need to get married because Marriage may not be for him. These five truths are:

1) Wives will think that you are always wrong.

2) Wives will always believe you are the cause of all relationship turmoil.

3) Wives will always follow Biological Imperative.

4) Wives do NOT like, nor want, sex as much as husbands do.

5) Wives will always strive to change their husbands.

These truths should be revered as holy. Anytime you contemplate taking an action that may affect your wife's life, thou shalt review the Five Wife Truths to ensure your actions do not clash with a time tested penta-truths. If you do take a moment to follow these procedures, you may save yourself some god-awful and wholly unnecessary ass-pain.

ALWAYS Respect the Five Wife Truths

1. *Wives will think that you are always wrong.*

Get ready for the harsh reality that you are just a guy, and as a guy, you are an idiot! You can be an expert computer programmer, psychology professor, or graduated top in your class at MIT, but your wife will think you're freak'in wrong whenever the two of you have a conflict. You'll be forced to try and explain what you mean until you're blue in the face but she still will not understand, nor capitulate... and you'll still be on the wrong side of every issue.

Wives have this disturbing habit of treating their husbands as though they are permanent fixtures. Wives act as though they do not have to worry, or try, to keep their husbands happy and satisfied because their husbands will *just, be there* in spite of how they are treated. Instead of treating husbands as friends, bad wives treat their husbands as subservient, inferior beings that are wrong anytime there is a disagreement.

Men aren't prepared for the standard faire of a girlfriend or wife second guessing them constantly. As a common example, wives will slowly begin to make comments about the driving habits of their husbands. This is despite the fact that you may have been driving years longer than she has, and you have far more driving experience and a better record than she does. She will still believe that she's a better driver than you are. You can be a full-time truck driver but once you get in that green Volvo of yours, your wife will still think you're clueless.

Wives would be better served to treat their husbands as FRIENDS (with benefits of course). Wives shall learn and understand that when friends treat each other well, they become best friends and can stay friends forever. When friends treat each other badly, friendships are lost because one friend will get sick of the other friends' bullshit and eventually realize they don't have to take it anymore.

Many wives should seriously contemplate whether their husbands would want to be friends with them if they were not married. I'd venture to say that if many men weren't legally bound to their wives, they'd be out of there faster than the wife can figure out what just happened. And, they are so self-centered that they would still blame the guy for not wanting to be around them.

Men don't like to talk about their own situations, but if you ask any married man *"about his friends"*, you'll find that most of their married buddies can't stand to hang around with their wives. It **cannot** merely be because all men are selfish, but it **can** be because wives stop being friendly and fun and somehow turn into bitchy micro-bosses that think they can order their husbands around. Husbands begin to feel as though they are stuck with their wives and stuck in their shitty marriages. Eventually, they just give up any goal of being happy and just accept that they have no chance for peace. Instead, they dream of escaping to freedom.

Put your Money into Peanut Butter

There is no more a stupefying thing that women do than take the judgment of others over that of the men they supposedly "love". The way this becomes annoyingly apparent is when the man suggests something and it is outright rejected by the wife. Amazingly, the idea is approved when the woman is prompted by someone else in her circle.

As an example, if a man told his wife that they should invest $4000 in peanut butter, the wife would immediately respond with a resounding **HELL NO**. This will last until her friend down the street, Seanna, suggests peanut butter is a great investment and that she and her husband are investing in it themselves. The wife will completely change her tune and support the peanut butter investment. The husband is left reminding the wife that he brought up the idea first.

Of course, the wife will do everything she can to somehow show that this is a different idea than hubby brought up. She must do this to ensure that hubby is never able to give a good idea about anything.

Eventually, you too will get annoyed by this and either accept the idea that your chick is not reasonable or you'll become upset by her and rebel the same way you did when you were 14 years old and your mother wanted you to study harder so you could be the President one day. Yes, wives will always think you're wrong. <u>If you cannot accept this truth..</u> <u>Marriage may not be for you.</u>

2. Wives will always believe you are the cause of all problems.

Nearly all humans are selfish by human nature. In a marriage, this concept is exaggerated to a new height. When you get married, you, as the man, must be prepared for the idea that YOU will be required to suck it up and take blame for everything that goes wrong in the world. If you don't take the blame you will solely be responsible for the turmoil that you've created.

Now obviously, marriages are relationships. Relationships require give and take from each participant. When one individual feels that he/she is doing more than the other spouse, there will naturally be tension. When one is getting good sex, and the other is not, there will be tension. Human nature demands that we do what we think is important before doing what others think is important.

What women do, however, is disregard the concept that the husband does things they believe are important in total. Wives are shocked and disgusted that it is not up to them to judge value and importance of every man's worldly decision. The most common example is one that millions of men from around the world suffer from; Watching sports! This pastime is important to 1.3721 Billion[33] men, but women think it's a waste of time. There are dozens of

---

[33] That statistic is not backed by fact. I just wanted to look official with a lot of footnotes.

examples just as basic and innocuous as this, where women attempt to assert their value on to their husband!

To avoid conflict, men have made it a point to "ask" wives, at first, for a little bit of peace. During sporting events, the dumb women interrupt and complain but the smart wives leave guys alone. Many wives do not want to accept this simple, insignificant thing and eventually the guy gets pissed off. And after dealing with this for a decade or so, a guy pushes her out of the way of the TV so he can watch a game and bam, *HE* gets arrested by the cops for spousal abuse. *That has never happened to me though...*

Standards and Double Standards

Wives have a standard for their men that would be wholly rejected if they had to live by the same standards themselves. A wife can call you lazy and you'd find it insulting, however, if you were to merely hint at your wife's laziness, not only her, but an army of women (femme-a-Nazis) -- that she will no doubt tell what you've just called her -- will be upset. Society in general would be up in arms and likely brand you a mental abuser for calling your bon-bon eating, do nothing, fat wife, "lazy".

The only person that would be on your side is Judge Judy. In principle, men would be on your side but if their wives are around, they won't say any words of support for fear their women will get all mad at them, not for daring share their opinions, but for disagreeing with them.

Wives create problems, but blame the guy when they do not get what they want. Guys; recognize you will always be the cause of all problems and understand that to a woman, you might as well be their child. You'll think it unfair but it will never matter. Even Ivana Trump dumped "The Donald", despite his awesomeness (what chance do you have?). Regardless of your job, a wife will always think that you are the cause of all turmoil. <u>If you cannot accept this truth.. Marriage may not be for you.</u>

3. Wives will always follow Biological Imperative.

We humans are still animals. We may be the smartest animals on the planet, but we are animals all the same. We humans are subject to certain rules of behavior that have helped our species survive to this point in our evolutionary history. Biological imperative is a constant factor through all species. In successful species, females want babies and males want females.[34] As humans, much of our life struggles stem from this recurring theme of women tricking men into having babies.

Wives want all of your money and man-juices to ensure the survival of the species. Women want to

---

[34] Unsuccessful species go extinct like the Dodo bird and eventually the stupid Pandas (yea, I said it). Quote me bastard!

nest, have a family, and fulfill the stupid little dreams they had when they were little girls. The guy, on the other hand, wants sex, a lot of sex, fun sex, and a diversity of sex, from numerous women. How much of a bummer is that? Sure, damn straight, it sucks, but it's not going to go away. Women can accept it; they can believe it's not part of the male makeup, or they can try to ignore this male biological imperative.

What does biological imperative make women do? Anything that Crack Cocaine or Crystal Methamphetamine will make women do. Specifically, biology makes women willing to lie, cheat, and steal to make their imperative happen. I'm sure we've all heard of those stories in which a lady went off the pill in order to trap a man by getting pregnant. We've also heard of women puncturing holes in their lovers rubbers. That actually happens, and yes, biology is a bitch! Now, I'm not calling (all) women bitches, but men, if you get married, there will be a point in which you will be calling your woman one.

Men also have biological imperatives we are attempting to fulfill and when the desire to be a good man clashes with the desire to bed any and all (most) women clash, the relationship with wives will also clash. Wives must understand and accept the nature of man. We strive and search to find freedom in all we do. Men dream of things that keep them on the move. This is why guys love nice vehicles, money, travel, and cheap whores (like wives used to be).

Coincidentally, this is why guys love the idea of being secret agents. Nothing about secret agents is permanent and it is the ultimate expression of freedom. Conversely, marriage is supposed to be permanent. It saps money, youth, and time. It means you won't travel and you're stuck with one woman, who is likely NOT acting like a whore. Would James Bond accept this? I think not! As a man getting married, or someone marrying a man, you have to comply with biological imperative. <u>If you cannot accept this truth.. Marriage may not be for you.</u>

4. Wives do not like sex as much as husbands do.

Just accept it! It's obviously the truth! You and I both know she doesn't want all of the kinky, dirty, shenanigans you fantasize about. Just forget all of that disgusting, sloppy stuff because it's not 'gonna happen again. Forget any new stuff you'd like to experiment with; that's not going to happen either. *If* you can manage to forget all of your quirky fantasies, you'll be a much happier man. The problem, however, is that *you can't forget about it*. Some of the best times in your life are your memories of those hot chicks you've (been telling people you've) hooked-up with back in the day.

Whether it be your high school days, college days, or your time in the Navy. If you can manage to dump those tasty, dirty stories, please let the rest of us dudes know how you did it. I cannot for the life of me forget my travels to Bangkok and, honestly, I wouldn't want to forget those memories if I could.

78

Your freaky memories are likely going to haunt you for the rest of your days.

Of course, your downfall will always be that you will always remember the good times and you cannot "un-remember" them. Those memories will torture and/or titillate you for the rest of your life. You cannot simply ignore the dirty deeds intertwined in your memories that have become part of your core being. Women may disagree but... whatever! With the exception of the sissiest (male feminists) amongst us, every man knows women do NOT like sex as much as men do, and wives are women too. Occasionally people make statements such as "women love sex as much as men do"... which is utterly ridiculous.

Oh sure, women and wives will come up with a story, anecdote, lie, or belief they can to prove to you that this is not true. The truth however is obvious. Women *CAN NOT* possibly love sex as much as men. They may love to have sex with the man they love[35], but men love sex so much, they'll get themselves in trouble thinking about it. Men cannot turn off their sex drive. We've all watched the TV show *Cops*. When is the last time you've seen a woman get arrested trying to pick up a male hooker? Why? Because there are no female *johns*. Get real!

You must come up with a way to suppress your memories of any sex that was better than your current girlfriend, wife, or future-wife. I find that alcohol works amazingly well! If it doesn't work for you, lie

---

[35] ...or the man that's paying them.

your ass off. NEVER admit to your chick what you've done in your past! Hide your true, hideous, *sexual* personality from your wife until you are 100% certain that she will be OK with it. <u>If you cannot accept this truth.. Marriage may not be for you.</u>

Your Sex life will go to hell!

You've heard guys say it for years, and that's because it's true. Occasionally, we are shocked when we hear a man say that "he's been married 15 years and his sex life is getting better".

There are those extremely lucky guys that have a girlfriend that is willing to try just about anything. Those are the extremely lucky dudes that most guys fantasize about being (you bastard!). Take it as a compliment and enjoy it while it lasts. But unless you're a swinger, your exciting sexual predicament is doomed to failure and you will eventually join the ranks of the rest of us horny, saddened husbands. You're hoping your sex life won't change, but inevitably, it will! We ALL think we'll be different, but alas, we NEVER are.

Curiously, women think that when the sex life goes bad, that the man has just lost interest in them. **This may be true**, but not for the reasons women "choose" to believe. They blame men because we've lost interest, but they NEVER want to accept responsibility from their side. The truth is that we've lost interest because they became supremely boring!

Women, I know it must be hard to hear, but if your man has lost interest, it's because you failed to keep things spicy. *It Is You!* Us men are simple, but for some reason, you are a turnoff! Again, I know it sucks for women to hear it, but maybe you've gotten a bit naggy, annoying, saggy, boring, sober, shrieky, conservative, picky, panicky, arrogant, clean, cautious, nosey, self-conscious, or yes, even fat! Put yourself under the microscope and ask, "what about you might be a turn-off to a guy?"

Most Men are laid-back, simple beasts that only require food, drink, a little attention, and "good booty". Note that I did NOT say "booty", but "GOOD booty". There is a difference! And if you didn't know there was a difference, well, there's your answer on what's causing problems in your relationship. Again, it's you! A woman cannot think they are a good companion merely because they can spread those legs and let the guy "do his thing", as though it is a great honor for the guy to be lucky enough to have sex with her.

Unfortunately, too many wives subscribe to this way of thinking. These are women who are shocked later when they find out that their man cheated on them. They ask, "*What did I do to deserve this?*" and they proclaim, "*I had sex with him whenever he wanted, why would he cheat on me?*" Many wives provide quantity when they should be more concerned with quality. It's the quality keeps men happy.

Yes, they did their "duty", but it wasn't good enough to keep him satisfied. The bottom line is that marriage changes sexual relationships. Not only will you understand the meaning of all of the jokes that people make about old married couples out there, but you will eventually understand that you will not be any different from those couples. Sex *may* be good when you are a newlywed. It wanes for a few years, and maybe it'll come back a tad bit after a few decades if you're lucky... or maybe it won't.

If you're really lucky, it won't come back and you'll move into a second bedroom and you and your wife will have sex on your birthdays and your anniversary (or whenever you get drunk). How lovely that'll be for you. Men and women must recognize this truth and accept that no good can come from the fact that women don't like sex as much as men do. Yet, that's what marriage will bring you. <u>If you cannot accept this truth.. Marriage may not be for you.</u>

5. *Wives will always change and want to change their husbands.*

It's said that sharks never sleep and I'll submit that wives will NEVER cease attempting to change husbands. This is the most important rule of the five. If you cannot successfully comply or accept this rule, how can any other rule be satisfied? You must understand that both a wife's actions and inactions are attempts to change your behavior. Wives understand that the longer they avoid an issue you care about it increases the odds that you'll eventually give up on your pursuits and just do what she wants so you don't have to listen to her. Women are not stupid, but they are like Nazi's moving into your house to seize control of your life.

Your relationship WILL change! It won't be changing in your favor either! You need to accept that despite any ideas that you've found the perfect girl, your future is NOT bright. The "perfect woman" is a mere illusion. And because of her fundamental need to change things. You *ARE* going to get screwed. We've all heard the saying:

> *"Men marry women because they don't want them to change, but women marry men to mold them into their dream man."*
>
> *Author Unknown*

It's nothing personal; we men are just wired differently. Men marry the women they like at that moment. Men would be extremely satisfied if their girlfriends didn't have a drastic mentality change once they became wives. Wives can get older and that's fine if they would just keep their youthful spirit. Men love girlfriends to be fun, exciting, hot, and sexy. Guys are not attracted to women that act like old ladies. Not even old dudes are attracted to that.

If you need further proof of this, just look at the women that married men have affairs with and/or leave their wives for. With the exception of a few notable anomalies, the newer chick is never more boring and less-attractive than the wives they replaced[36].

Now, I haven't collected statistics or anything, but surely you can accept that if a guy is married and  has a girlfriend on the side, that girlfriend is NOT more boring or naggy than the woman the guy is married to. This explains why some married men sometimes have girlfriends; they don't want to deal with the attitudes their wives saddle upon them. Women, on the other hand, marry men because they see visions of their futures.

Not only is their boyfriend becoming their husband, but, women will immediately see visions of huge weddings and extravagant honeymoons dancing in their heads (even on their first dates). A wife's perspective changes literally overnight. It no longer is about fun or dating; it's about their wedding days. And they'll get you into trouble and then blame you if things don't work out the way they envisioned. As an example of this curiosity, men (you will too) regularly get bullied or coerced into buying houses and having children because of your dreams that it is possible to keep wives happy. You must learn that **_YOU CANNOT_**

---

[36] With the exception of that one horse-faced lady that rode off with Princess Diana's husband. Who knows what that was about.

SATISFY A WIFES FANTASY. They are far too selfish for that and they will not be willing to listen to you. Accept it!

It will inevitably bring tension when the wife perceives that the husband is not doing enough to support her wifely vision of home ownership or parenting. Every bit of tension or disagreement becomes the fault of the husband, which is totally bullshit since it was the wife that led him to all of the chaos in the first place. Your wife doesn't like you as you are and wants to "perfect" you and if you cannot accept this truth.. Marriage may not be for you.

You've reviewed The Five Wife Truths and perhaps you've gained some insight. It is time to take a quiz to determine your ability to respect the Five Truths. Answer honestly because you'll only hurt yourself if you deny the truth and lie. You should care enough about your future that you will be truthful. No one else matters.

Marriage Quiz

1) Are you happy with your freedom as a single person?
   - a. I'm totally happy single!
   - b. Marriage makes me nervous.
   - c. Marriage will make me happier.

2) How many, and when, will you have children?
   - a. We disagree but it'll work out.
   - b. We already agreed on numbers.
   - c. Hasn't come up yet.

3) Do you need or want a Pre-nuptial agreement?
   - a. We don't need or want one.
   - b. She won't sign it!
   - c. I'm afraid to ask.

4) How often will you have sex? (per week, month)
   - a. We drink a lot! It's not a problem.
   - b. We'll go with the flow.
   - c. Who knows? Not looking good though!

5) Can you stay faithful to one lover?
   - a. I will give it my best shot! (or shots)
   - b. No one else wants me... so yes.
   - c. What? I 'gotta stay faithful?

6) Do you and your fiancé (or whatever) both define "cheating" similarly?
   - a. We see eye-to-eye on cheating.
   - b. We'll know it when we see it.
   - c. She thinks "looking" is cheating!

Scoring Key

Give yourself 3 points for each "a" answer, 2 points for each "b" answer, and 1 point for each "c" answer.

Write your score here _____

If you got 6 – 9 / Definitely NOT ready. You are not showing the characteristics of a person who should get married. You'll end up as a spousal abuser, or you'll get busted cheating. You are not smart enough and it seems as though you lack common sense. On a positive note, you will grow up and change over time but for now, don't do it!

If you got 10 – 14 / If you marry, it'll last awhile but you'll be unhappy most of the time. Unfortunately, this is where most married men lie. You may get to the point where you give up your hopes of dreams so your marriage can last a tad-bit longer. But you'll never really be satisfied. You'll probably have a couple of affairs given the opportunity[37]. But hey, at least you'll be in the group of marriages considered "average".

If you got 15 – 18 / Good for you. You might last a few of decades (which is all we can ask for). Marriage is a good risk for you and it sounds like you gave

---

[37] Or maybe your woman will have the affairs. Who knows? Whatever!

reasonable and realistic answers. But, look at the bright side, even if this first marriage doesn't work out for you, your second go around will be more stable because you'll contemplate why your marriage failed. You probably won't make the same wife selection mistakes the next time around.

Do I really need to remind you again

Cut your answers out and burn them. *Do NOT let your chick see these last few pages if you have any inclination for self-preservation... Especially if you're already married!*

Cheat'in Hearts

> *"It isn't tying himself to one woman that a man dreads when he thinks of marrying; it's separating himself from all the others."*
>
> *Helen Rowland*

Alright, I have to be careful of what I say here so as to not come off sounding like I'm in any way pushing or supporting the act of cheating. I add this section to help you understand why many married men (and women) actually end up finding a little action outside of their relationships. I am NOT giving directions. If you decide to step out on your marriage (cheat), you must realize that you are solely responsible for your actions. There's no one to point to, and no one to blame. You did it!

I further add this section because if you get caught cheating, you should at least want to avoid leaving a swath of anger and devastation in your wake. We all know that morally, what you're doing is probably wrong. But why get caught if you don't have to? Just because you're a dirtbag doesn't mean you have to be a discredited dirtbag!

Don't be too hard on yourself!

It is human nature that you WILL have to fight the temptation to step out because, well... you're a man. Again, I don't say this to grant permission, but to be truthful concerning **male** biological imperative. Men want women. More accurately, men want every woman they see. It is not only a human condition, its all animals, even Swans and Wolves. These are animals whom we humans romanticize as being loyal and monogamous for life. Even amongst these species, there is regular cheating going on.

In nature, this is called: EPC, or Extra Pair Copulation. To understand why this is a natural factor, you will have to understand that in nature the accepted rule is, survival of the fittest. Females get more, and better quality genetic material[38], while males get more (quantity) sex and have better odds at inseminating females in order to produce more healthy offspring. It is pure biology and nothing more!

Now open marriages seem to work for some and swingers have been saying "the couple that swings together, stays together" since the 70's. Now, I don't know

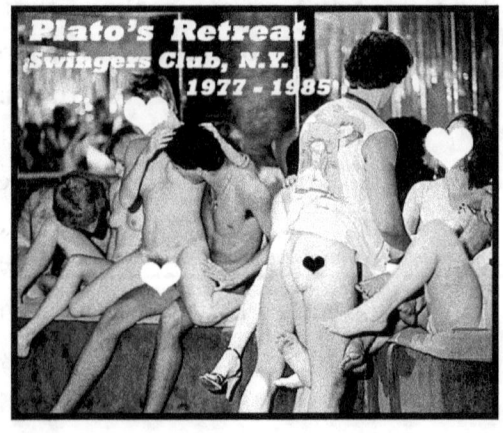

---

[38] By this, we mean better biological juices. Semen, Spooge, Cum... I just wanted to write these words in a book.

if that's true (although it's definitely fascinating) but I will say that if you don't think you're capable of being monogamous and your Fiancé expects it, you two probably shouldn't marry each other.

This section may seem cold and callous but with both sexes doing their parts, they ensure the success and survival of the species. Darwin (apparently) was right! That said, there are 2 absolute rules of behavior that both spouses shall always be aware of. One is for the wife/woman, and the other, the husband/man. The rules are:

1) The Rule Of Any-Girl (for women)
2) The Rule Of MAD (for men)

The Rule Of Any-Girl

This is an absolute rule for wives and is pretty damned simple really, *even* for women to understand. This rule reminds women that if they aren't willing to keep their men satisfied, they must be prepared for what will follow. It recognizes the needs of men and illuminates it in a way that women can quickly understand and comply with if they so choose. As a man, you should make sure any woman you marry accepts the premise of "The Rule of Any-Girl".

If you happen to be a woman and reading this book, please skip to the next chapter. I'm sure you'll be offended if you choose to read beyond this point. But I have to say it anyway. The rule states succinctly:

> *Wives better be willing to do what Any-Girl on the street will do sexually, or else, Husbands will go find, Any-Girl on the street to do what their wives aren't willing to do.*

If a man is happy, he will keep his wife happy. Wives are quick to blame husbands when their relationships start to go to hell but perhaps wives need to look at themselves a bit more to determine if they are also – just a bit – responsible for the activities of their spouses. Before you say "no", complain under your breath, and disregard this idea, recognize the fallacy that when a woman is not happy in her marriage, it's a given to her, and society, that her **husband must somehow be responsible**.

And yet; when a man is not happy in his marriage, wives will also suggest that it's also **his own flaw and he is responsible**. The wife is in no way "ever", a problem. As a man, understand that in the absence of a wifely sex-tape scandal, you will always be considered responsible for the marriage failing. It may be unfair but this is how the world works.

Although, daytime TV shows have been making people laugh for years by exploiting the foibles of man, many people would say that I should avoid this topic because it might tempt honest men into cheating. That's just a stupid thing to say! If you put an open cash register in front of a bank robber, he's going to go for the easy score. Now, if you put an honest man in front of that same open cash register, he would not snatch any money and would likely inform you of your error. The reason men cheat is inadequate women. There, I said it!

Women must be warned to ensure their man is content so he'll never stray. If women disregard his needs and desires, they are practically forcing him to cheat.

Men know they should avoid this urge because it's NEVER cool, but men, for the love of the gods, if you do choose to tomcat around, give yourself some basic framework to minimize the risks. Let's be clear! I'm not endorsing your cheating lifestyle (you bastard), but I don't want a bunch of wives getting hurt by you dudes because you're a bunch of idiots.

The Rule Of Mutually Assured Discretion

Men, during the Cold War, the US strategy to thwart a nuclear attack from the Soviet Union was MAD, or Mutually Assured **Destruction**. The thinking was that if the Ruskies attacked us with Ballistic Nuclear Missiles, we would launch our missiles back. Both countries would be annihilated and thus, it was not worth the risk for either side to attack the other because he would surely be destroyed... and the other party knew it. MAD kept both sides at bay, and kept friskiness in check through fear.

If you're a cheating bastard, MAD applies to you also. For you, it is Mutually Assured **Discretion**. As a married man, you'll be excited that anyone wants you. Your standards are pretty low but you must not let the excitement that someone still finds you attractive cloud you moral compass. Stay strong! What bachelors never understand is that after a few years of marriage, you'll become a **beggar and not a chooser**. You will be so excited that someone "wants" you, that you're at severe risk of making a stupid mistake. You'll take the scraps. But even as the old and lonely beggar-boy you will become, you must follow the basic concept that you:

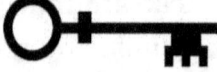

Never mess around with anyone who doesn't have as much to lose as you.

What does this mean? This means stay away from those single girls. Unless you're in Thailand, Vegas, or possibly, Constantinople[39]. What would a single, or ugly girl care if she told anyone that she slept with some dirtbag like you? Nothing! She's likely proud that a, no doubt, older man whom she, for some crazy reason believes is filthy rich[40], likes

---

[39] Oh My God! Really? Istanbul, Turkey. You really have to go back to school and get some education.

[40] You dirty deceitful liar!

her. She won't care who knows! Just ask Monica Lewinski (not that she's particularly fat). Your fat, hairy chick[41] will tell all of her fat and ugly friends. She'll even post cell phone pics of you all over the internet. She has zero reason to be discreet. And it'll all be because you couldn't follow this basic tenant.

Now, on the flipside, imagine your married counterpart. She has just as much vested interest in discretion as you do. She understands that her hairy-backed, Bud-drinking, tiny-peckered, slob husband will (no doubt) beat her if he finds out about her extracurricular activities. And she's embarrassed she touched your ugly-ass in the first place. You're ugly!

Too many guys have been brought down, not because they are cheating bastards, but because they failed to follow this simple rule. This isn't the 1800's. If you are caught, and your wife is dumb enough to stay with your stupid ass, you will never live it down. Don't get caught! And the only way to do that... is to NOT cheat. So choose a wife **wisely** and if you must cheat, choose your Jezebel **even more** wisely.

Once your sex life starts to deteriorate, the intimacy and marriage will follow until it withers away. You are along for the ride during the withering process. Poor Bastards! Just accept that wives and marriage will wear you down to the point you want to pull out your "Strang'lin Gloves".

---

[41] How many fat chicks have gotten lucky with a guy who was just feeling kinda horn-doggedy? ...Not that I've ever done that [uncomfortable chuckle]!

Remember John Edwards!

Yes, you may know him as a Presidential candidate but many people know him as "The Dumb-Ass". He was cheating on his wife with a lady who started their relationship with the statement, "You're so hot". This was a dead giveaway that she wanted to get in his pants but, if Johnny followed the rules, he would not have fallen for her slutty charms.

If he recognized that she didn't have as much to lose as he did and avoided her, he wouldn't have had to worry about being alone with her or about any flirting because she would have been deemed *off-limits*. He wouldn't have had to worry about her getting pregnant, or destroying his reputation and political career because; He would've stayed away from her because that was the rule. And to talk about hurting your family, remember, he did all of this while his wife was recovering from cancer. What a Slimy Dirtbag! And then to top it off, the chick got pregnant. Ouch!

Don't be a John Edwards! [42]

---

[42] Doesn't he just look like a slimy douchebag? Seriously?

Obviously, not everyone cheats, but I don't know why any woman would think that she's immune to such a possibility; especially if she admits that she **can** be kind of a bitch sometimes. Women must accept their responsibilities to ensure that their husbands never even get the urge to stray. If you cannot help your lady understand that, all is lost!

It is the greatest irony ever that the guys that don't have the urge to cheat, are largely composed of those dudes who are married to the wild ladies who keep them excited and titillated both in bed, and in life. The guy is kept on his toes, and just does not want to cheat. Unfortunately, these wild women are likely the cheaters in that relationship. What does this mean? If you're a man and you're not cheating, your wife probably is! But not to worry, it is all part of life's rich pageantry.

Although you'll hear older couples say their sex lives got better over time, these are usually situations that stem around generational differences. These are the older couples that have stuck to the old faithful *Missionary* position for 40 plus years and just realized they could try other things. Of course these new Kama Sutra-esque positions made sex better for them.

What you are risking

I would be remiss if I failed to warn you of what your behavior could bring. You have to know that if you choose to cheat and your little secret is discovered, you will likely end up divorced, not living with your kids, in a small apartment by yourself, lonely, and methamphetamine addicted. But the worse thing is that you may hurt the person you love... I assume you kinda "love" your spouse since you haven't divorced her ass already.

So the bottom line of this section is to remind you of the consequences your infidelity will likely have if you are busted. Men, in general, have always, and will always cheat despite the byproduct of likely hurting their spouse. So ignoring the emotional stuff, the real ramifications will be that you'll catch an STD or get some harlot[43] pregnant.

You can catch an S-T-D or a K-I-D

Like John Edwards, and millions of men that have come before you, you may end up with a K-I-D out of wedlock by the woman you cheated on your wife with. You will become some *harlot's* baby-daddy. In that very moment you become a baby-daddy, you'll find yourself in that same class of men on any given Jerry Springer episode. And you don't want to be like that guy. Almost instantaneously, women will label you a scumbag and you'll have to work extra hard to explore random hoochie-boobs.

If you don't catch a K-I-D, you might catch an S-T-D like that one famous rocker who shared Hepatitis with that famously big-boobed, blonde chick, that was not particularly hot, but modeled and couldn't really act, yet still made millions of bucks

---

[43] Harlot?! Nice!, I'm bringing that word back!

acting only to go spectacularly broke. You don't want to be that guy either!

The sad part of all of this is that If you marry, you'll learn not to be too judgmental of other married men... because you'll know exactly why any number of men felt that irrational or unbecoming behavior is the way out. Still some (mostly women), will just suggest that if a man's not happy, he should just get a divorce. This is too simple of an answer. Marriage involves items such as finances, property, children, and not being able to survive without a second income. Factors such as these make it a serious decision on whether to leave or not. **Marriage is truly the modern form of the ball and chain.**

If you get married, you have to be in it 100% or you'll never be content. But to be content, you must choose wisely or nothing but trouble will follow you. Marriage is just insufferable. BE VERY CAREFUL and determine what you're willing to risk before you take the gamble. If you get to this point, remember as a general rule, cheating leads to only bad stuff... unless you're European. Think or you'll wake up to find you're someone you don't want to be. Find the right person for you.

5

Last Train to Splitsville

> *"I never even believed in divorce until after I got married."*
>
> *Diane Ford*

In the end, it's harder to get out of a marriage than to get into one. To get married in America today all you need to do is go to a Justice of the Peace, pay a fee, possibly get a blood test, and voila; you're married! All-in-all, it could take as little as 2 days (if you're in Vegas). You say your name, and say "I do".

To get a Divorce on the other hand; that could cost you big money and this is seemingly by design. It could take years if money is involved. "Someone" wants to make it extremely hard to get out of a marriage. Not to be one of those conspiracy theory guys, but I blame the Global Warming... And possibly, my man George Bush[44].

Religious people would say it's because of evil; Intellectuals would say it's because of knowledge; Philosophers would say it's just a function of life; and realists would say nothing lasts forever! I say they're all freaking idiots! The math just doesn't add up.

Marriage itself became common when people's life spans averaged about 36 years. Now though, people live 80 to 90 years and sometimes even a few years longer. Does it mean that if you get married at 25[45], that it is reasonable you should just be stuck until you (or your spouse) gives up the ghost and parts way with life? You say yes, but why? Could it be that, just maybe, marriages are exactly like life and every other relationship you've ever had? *All* relationships go through a cycle and *most*

---

[44] Since some idiot's continue to blame him for everything!

[45] Which is still way too F-ing young.

relationships end, just like life! Unless you live in a town of 200 inbred yokels, you are most likely NOT going to be adult friends with the people you called friends when you were playing dodge-ball back in elementary school! Relationships, just like life, naturally wither away and die.

We all have those depressing friends that are "stuck" in a marriage that they incessantly complain about. We find that we constantly tell them to just leave; but you'll learn just as your friend has, that it's not that easy! If it were, dudes would be dumping wives like they dump doo-doo's. Unfortunately, you cannot learn this before you get married. You are going to lose out also if, and when, you get married. Your mamma told you that you were special, but you're not. You're just another swing'in schlong!

The Guy "Always" Loses Out

There are a couple of truths about divorces. It may be unfortunate, but listen to this because you must be prepared for this inevitability. When a divorce is coming, the law is [just a tad] more favorable to women due to their biological role as the birth-givers and nurturers. Shocking, huh? Divorce is going to be rough on the man due to their "traditional role" as head of the household and primary breadwinner, however unfortunate.

It is even more unfortunate because nowadays, many wives make far more money than their husbands, and yet, the guy can still expect to lose half of his shit, along with his kids when there is a split.

Now as a single or recently married guy, I know you didn't plan on having the kid(s). But you wanted one eventually anyways. So let's just presume that you didn't take enough effort to NOT have the little rug-rats and now that they are here, you're his or her "da-da". If you are honorable at all, you'll recognize that you're in it for life. You are tied to that bloody ex-wife bitch forever despite how much you may eventually hate and despise her. On a positive note, you will come to love those kids you've created.

The bottom line is that you'll want to be around the kids, yet avoid the wife. You won't be able to figure out how to do that. You'll have created life, presuming those kids are yours, and you'll have a need and responsibility to ensure that life you've created is thriving. The law is definitely pointed against the guy. Unless your wife is a crack-head, you might as well write off the idea of getting custody. Your ex-wife can, and will, make your life miserable regardless.

You'll have to be friendly for the sake of your kids and if you don't, statistics suggest that your kids will be just as unhappy as you were when you were married to that chick. Don't take them down with you. Be careful!

True Marriage Snippet (in 188 characters):
Paul asked Terrance, a co-workers, why he doesn't have a picture of his wife on his desk next to the photos of his children. Terrance answered that it was because "wives were temporary". Ouch!

It's cheaper to keep her!

No doubt you've heard the term, "Cheaper To Keep Her". What this means is that men are in a position where they realize that if they get a divorce they will still have to pay for the kids, their education, their hobbies, their new bachelor household, and also, a place where their soon-to-be ex-wife will live[46]. This does not take into account how much they'll lose in the divorce itself. So the next time you wonder why so many married men are in marriages they hate, this should be your prime suspect!

Getting a divorce is much more of a financial drain than being unhappy in your marriage. Many suggest that empty nest syndrome is why there are a high number of divorces when the kids move out. I would suggest that many men will wait until their kids are 18 years old and out of the house before they head out of their unhappy living conditions.

Just remember that anyone can get a divorce. Most of us aren't as glamorous as Liz Taylor, crazy as Mike Tyson[47], violently unstable as Mel Gibson, athletic as Michael Jordan, as appealing as Brooke Shields, rich as Donald Trump, or as open and honest as Hugh Hefner. And yet, all of these people are members of the not-so-exclusive divorce club and actually some of them multiple times.

---

[46] Don't be a deadbeat. That's not cool!

[47] Not that I don't respect Mr. Tyson. I supremely don't want any trouble from him.

> *"Three rings of marriage are the engagement ring, the wedding ring, and the suffering."*
>
> *Author Unknown*

So what can a single man take away from this book to ensure that **IF** he chooses to get married, that he increases the odds of a successful marriage. He should learn that if a dude is dumb enough to absorb this information and still get married, he's an idiot. But I'll implore him to follow the three **take-aways** below and use them to his benefit. They will save him if he contemplates their true value prior to any marriage proposals:

1. A Prenup
2. Live with her first.
3. Just don't do it.

I know it's hard for you to come to a snap conclusion at the moment because you're a bit nervous about the prospect of marriage to begin with. You know that if you marry the wrong person you can literally mess up your life. But you don't want to listen to people telling you what NOT to do. **You Are Right!** Your marriage is your decision. You can do what you want but, *will it really hurt anything if you just listen to the concerns of those around you?* Do what you have to do in order to protect yourself from a crazy wife. You'll only save yourself and save your own future.

Go For The Pre-Nup

 Use some common sense. Many people will suggest that you only use a prenup as an underhanded scheme to get out of a marriage if you need to. Many women are beginning to understand this and will sign one readily [because of biological imperative]. But don't make the stupid mistake of basing prenup conditions on your inflated "FUTURE" value and earnings.

The problem with your expectations of your future goals and earning potential is that, now a days, your woman could very well out-earn your piddly "burger-flipping" income with her Lawyer pay. You would have just screwed yourself out of half of her stuff because you forced her to sign a pre-nup when you thought you were going to make it big as a rock icon, commodities trader, or fast-food magnate.

If you or your family is wealthy like the Kennedy's and your slutty, former-hooker girlfriend isn't rich, you *NEED* a Pre-Nup. If your chick is not willing to sign one, DO NOT marry her. Marriages fail all of the time and if you do take the plunge with this woman you *THINK* you love, you'll end up losing half of all the useless "stuff" you think makes you happy. If you look into yourself; you know I'm right! You're not attractive; she just wants your money.

Your pre-nup will serve a purpose and protect both parties for a few years but it is no way a guarantee in a court of law. Especially after you get caught cheating... and the Judge is a lady... and she's been cheated on before. But it does show your intent.

Live with her first

 The second thing you can do to avoid a crappy marriage and devastating divorce is to simply live with her first. I know you're all super-religious (or at least your wife is), and you haven't been to Church in a couple of decades. But your wife may turn out to be a devout, crazy, or super anal[48] (retentive). You might want to know if she's gonna harass you into going to church every week or if she wants to eat dinner at a table every night with the TV off. There are too many areas that should not be left to fate. She could be a vampire, and you should know that kind of thing.

You're already going to have ongoing problems with her calling you disgusting for NOT picking up your funky chonies or drizzling urine all over the toilet seat. Why let her unnecessary and incessant nagging catch you off guard. The unfortunate truth is that:

You'll never know someone until you live with them and, when you live with them you may find you don't want to know them.

---

[48] Yea Right! Forget about that, you're getting married now.

How can you possibly know basic information like where the other person wants to live and retire? If you want to make downtown NY your home, while she wants white picket fences in Kansas, someone has to give up and give way. And you can only know this type of information by living with each other first.

Does it make sense that you would put yourself in a permanent position without trying it out temporarily first? Women have this saying that us guys should understand and accept as a set-in-stone fact. Women say, *"Why would he buy the cow[49] if he can get the milk for free"?* I'm suggesting that you already know the truth here! Ask yourself:

Would you buy a car before you test-drive it?

Obviously NOT! **Live with her first!** Have sex with her first! Don't be a fucking-idiot. Don't get buyer's remorse when you could've tested out the product before you went all out.

Just Don't Do It.

Now, I've already said it about 33 times, but the only way you can 100% protect yourself is if you, just don't do It! Marriage will lead you to nothing but trouble. Knowledge and wisdom will lead you to understand

---

[49] Which I think is hilarious when women use this.

that marriage is not the answer for you, it is the problem that you're heading towards.

Remember what I told you about (1) Biological Imperative and (2) the Marriadox. Individually, these would be reasons to avoid marriage; however, when mixed together in the same woman, you get an entirely new beast. Your girl could have some serious issues, and yet, you are still willing to get your ass married. Your lady could be a selfish, money grubbing, slut, but you don't seem to care and you're not willing to accept the clues she's throwing you. You will eventually hit a "Tipping Point".

In a marriage, that Tipping Point is when the bad shit of the marriage outweighs the good shit. This is akin to the point of no return in which it becomes easier to go forward to the destination than to turn around and try to go home to your origin. The typical tipping point in a marriage usually involves infidelity or threats of violence.

If you get married and your wife ever says she's going to poison your porridge, the marriage is pretty much over. If you ever threaten to kill your wife, if she's smart, she'll believe you and leave that quickly. It is important to listen to what a spouse says. Tipping points may not be as dramatic as poison but they are obvious indicators when one should realize that the marriage is over. You cannot stop the inevitable. Just don't get married; and you'll never reach any tipping points.

I understand that merely giving someone the advice, **"Just Don't Do It"** will not work in the real world because it's like throwing a grenade into a room; people's instinct takes over and they just run. They don't really learn anything when they're running, but it is important to understand the man's thought process works nearly the same. It is the same reason young boys will look you square in the eyes, and throw something even though you warned them that they would get a spanking if they did throw it. It's just in their nature.

Every year, millions of Salmon around the world get the urge to procreate (just because their

parents tell them to probably). They fight their way around rocks, swim against the rushing water, jump up white water rapids, avoid stupid fishermen, and swim through a gauntlet of bears trying to rip their skin off. Do they do this for money? No! They go through all of this just to make it to a lake so they can fertilize a few hundred eggs... and then immediately die of exhaustion. Why would they go through all of this? Stupidity? Sadly, man and Salmon think alike. And just like those stupid fish, men are swimming upstream[50].

---

[50] Just because they are "supposed to"

Disadvantage = Man

You'll have to apply some Sun Tzu-like strategy when competing against the will of a woman. In general, men are not prepared with the information they need to beat a woman at a game she is biologically given an obvious advantage[51] but there are several **Avoiding Marriage Strategies (AMS)** you can follow that will help you put up the good fight in your efforts to avoid marriage. They are:

AMS-1: *Tell her immediately when she does something that doesn't work for you.*

AMS-2: *Introduce your would-be Fiancé to your family and friends.*

AMS-3: *Be yourself always; No matter what!*

AMS-4: *Take People as they come to you; always!*

It would seem ironic that despite how much I provide you methods to avoid marriage that if you can adhere to these strategies, you actually improve your odds of finding a person that is best matched for you. Let's review these strategies:

---

[51] ... Women have a crotch-goddess that most men worship. Yes! The goddess rules the nether region between female legs and thighs.

Tell her immediately when...

Most marital[52] issues stem from communication problems. Although poll after poll, and statistic after study, have concluded that couples have arguments, divorces, and conflicts over money, distrust, and withholding of attention and/or affection, these themes are usually symptoms of the greater issue of interpersonal-communications.

You must have respect for those whom you deal with in order to be honest with them. Obviously, you might want to be a bit tactful, but the goal of living with another human should be to communicate effectively with them. _WHEN_ you run into a situation where confusion arises [and you will], you must understand that you are in jeopardy of being misunderstood to the point that any word you say can be further misconstrued, thus leading you into a heinous argument. Watch what you say because once words leave your mouth, they will likely come back to haunt you for decades.

With that said, you must learn to immediately inform a girlfriend or wife when she does something that doesn't work for you. If she does not know there is a problem, she cannot fix it. Communication is meant to put you both on notice that you don't like a circumstance. And if she doesn't choose to change,

---

[52] And problems of the world from business to international relations

then you also have information you need to make educated future decisions.

It is difficult because wives change and intentionally try to manipulate husbands. But from the male perspective, it is important that you halt her immediately when things don't work for you. If you don't fail at this, she will continue to do the offending action. If informing her just doesn't work, you'll have to make a decision to either accept it or not. You can always pick up and leave if it's that important to you. There will come a point when it's not her fault, but really, your problem to deal with.

 ### *Introduce her to your family and friends NOW!*

There is a tendency with men to keep our new girlfriends away from our families as we start dating. The reasoning is that we don't want to introduce someone that might one day become a serious girlfriend or wife to a bunch of crazy people (your family) that might ruin it or scare her away. But that thinking is ass-backward.

The moment you get a chick and things start getting serious, you should throw her in the fire (not real fire) and introduce her to your family. Specifically your mother and sisters if you have them; why? Because mothers and sisters are judgmental as hell. Women will say the things that you are thinking directly to the woman you're trying to get serious with. Your chick needs to hear your concerns and since you don't have the cajones (balls/nuggets/kick-targets) to say anything, let your family take care of it.

Listen to what your family and friends say about your chick because, in theory, they want what is best for you and they don't have the luxury of being intimate or caring what your would-be spouse might think. They will call a duck, a duck, or in this case; They will call a bitch, a bitch! *Introduce them all, and let family and friends ruthlessly sort them out!*

 ### *Be Yourself Always; No Matter What.*

Be Yourself! If you act like someone else and you portray your thoughts and ideas differently than you actually feel, you will find that you'll have to live a lie that's hard to extricate yourself from. If you build a relationship on that lie, you will have to cover up your lies with other lies until you are forced to accept that houses built on deceit all eventually collapse.

Whatever makes you the *used-condom* you are, is what you should portray. If you like wearing tighty-whities, wear them. If you like sardines, eat them. If you smoke when you drink, go ahead and smoke when you drink. If you're a pervert who likes to be slightly spanked with shoes and forced to lick feet, make it known. Be yourself or you will have to hide all of your behaviors that you hid from her initially. That is no way to live! Imagine having to go a lifetime without licking feet when all you had to do was be honest up front and meet the right person for you.

You could've been in foot-licking heaven, but instead you're married to a puritan.

Many divorces are triggered when couples are forced to come to grips when one spouse "changes". We always hear about someone (usually a wife) turning to their spouse and declaring, *"You've Changed! Now you're just a real bastard[53]!"* The real story is that most guys probably don't "change" all that much. The problem is that when guys are dating, they hide their true personality up front because, well, the girl was allowing him to touch her boobs and a guy never wants to mess up that arrangement with a bunch of tiny, sordid details.

The most important reason you should always be yourself is that, getting a divorce because you've *changed* is partially your own fault. You will bear *some* responsibility for getting yourself into a relationship when you weren't being authentic. I know you might find it a tad bit shocking to learn that while you aren't honest when meeting a chick, she isn't either when meeting the likes of you. You must sort through the lies like you're a Private investigator if you hope to identify her real personality.

Hopefully, if you act like yourself when you meet a woman, she'll be repulsed by your honesty and walk away from your ass. Your problem; averted!

---

[53] I actually saw this go down in public once. And yes, it was as hilarious as it sounds.

Take People As They Come

Life is too short to waste time on attempting to decipher people unless you're getting paid for it. You should always take people as they come because, they are telling you what they are. They are giving you free information and they are possibly even giving you warning signs.

If a woman seems to be shady, treat her like she's shady. If she's a vegetarian, treat her as a vegetarian. If she's bitchy or seems like she had a bad childhood, don't think that she'll ever change. Accept her as she is and make a decision to deal with it or get away while the getting's good.

Getting to know someone is a tough job and if they're trying to impress you, it'll take 3 times as long to get to know them.

When it comes to taking people as they are, the problem with women is that they are anti-man, and they want you to do everything that is "anti-man". Women strive to change men into something they are not. When a man allows this to happen for whatever reason, he drastically decreases the likelihood of his own happiness. Conversely he also increases the odds of divorce. Why? Because he cannot hide his disgusting and disturbing true-self forever. One day he will realize that only the truth will set him free. He will also realize that trying to keep his wife happy is such a useless prospect, that it is not logical to continue attempting such a monumental scam.

It would have been much cleaner and simpler of a solution to be honest from the first meeting. You should learn who **YOU** are before you attempt to date anyone; even if that means you don't get to see her ***mustn't-touch-it***[54] (her goods).

And Now Then,

We've reviewed the four, Avoiding Marriage Strategies (AMS), and you should gather that these

rules will not only help you stay away from marriage, but on the flipside, these strategies will weed out the weak women that will only cause you problems. If you are able to follow these simple rules, you are more likely to meet someone that is a match for you and your hideous personality.

---

[54]The word "Mustn't" is a contraction of the words "Must Not". The first known usages were in the year 1741. Puritan/Victorian Mothers would teach their daughters that their Coochies were called "mustn't-touch-it's". How creepy is that? but you come to learn about marriage, and you also learn about English. You're welcome!!

6

Why Some Marriages Work

> *"All marriages are happy. It's the living together afterward that causes all the trouble."*
>
> *Raymond Hull*

It may be surprising, but some marriages actually do work. Many of us folk who have been married understand just how complicated working marriages are but, the single souls amongst us cannot possibly comprehend the intricacies since they have not been so blessed. This is the only saving grace for marriage as an institution that the ignorant will get married despite the fact that they know it sucks.

Single people are like Nazi's. They know getting married is wrong and yet they do it anyway and say they're just following orders (not in those words). (1) They don't know why they're doing it, (2) They can't explain the big picture, (3) the government wants them to do it, and (4) you must conform with the will of society. Yet, men will still marry.

The future of marriage is sustained in the irrational beliefs, blissful ignorance, and innocent delusions of those who would someday marry.

But first, let us ask, what is a healthy marriage? Who the fuck knows? Every book you (probably not you) have read on marriage describes this magical type of keyword-filled relationship where both parties can resolve their differences fairly, with compromise, with compassion, and empathy for the other spouse, and with elusive, and effortless communication that address' the needs of the spouse.

This magic relationship described by other books is based on the fact that the couple "loves" each other. Of course, you know that the love thing is bullshit based on our discussion earlier in the book. The biggest fault with these books is their belief in a supreme formula that can create, shape, and mold a great marriage. Hey, don't get pissed off at me! Just understand that if there was such a formula, the hundreds of books that are published every year on building a better marriage, would be made obsolete because everyone would be able to apply the one formula. But alas, that is pure horse boo boo!

Not that I should have to say this again as it should be obvious, but there is NO magic formula that works for everyone. We can only look at some of the circumstances that help *some* couples work together to build a strong relationship. As we put the microscope to them, we see that all of these relationships... are boring as hell! If you are a boring person, your odds of a long marriage are apparently pretty great. Two people with a lack of personality are a match made in boring-ass heaven and can stay together for years; so long as they both stay boring.

Every once in awhile, you hear that story of a couple that has been married for 50 years or more. Everyone within earshot always shares an "awww moment". If you're like me, you'd hear that and say something to the effect of, "Damn, that sucks for him!" Just knowing that he gave up on all of his life's dreams, ambitions, and goals for a half of a century makes me think, "Wow, that poor bastard"!

Now, hey, I'm not trying to start a fight or get stalked by some women's group, but look; wives spend your money, rag your ass, and that's pretty much all. If you're okay with that... go to town! Give her the ring and tie that knot! But it's educational to note why these marriages work over 40 or 50 years.

So far we've discussed items that you need to worry about in order to avoid marriage, but I haven't given any ideas men can use in order to have "healthy marriages"[55]. There are some things you can do, but you must recognize that marriages last longest when (1) Roles are definitive, and (2) someone gives up on their dreams and goals.

The majority of humans live in a pattern. They get into a groove and that's all they require. So long as they have their role as the breadwinner, or home-maker, mother, father, they can do it for decades; day after day, month after month. If a couple cannot build their grooves and patterns, they will fight chaos as well as each other until a divorce occurs.

After all I've said about successful marriages, the key message to take away is that marriages work when two people see things the same or extremely similar. If a couple is not on the same page, they are doomed to failure. When you're struggling to act like you're asleep next to your new wife, just remember when your non-crazy friends and family were telling you NOT to get married. Remember them telling you

---

[55] There may be such a thing, but I know very few that qualify. Mostly, problems are just hidden from those outside of the marriage.

that you're making a dreadful mistake and to think about it a bit more. You thought they didn't know what they were talking about but now you see their wisdom.

Also listen to those who know you when they tell you to get out of the marriage as well. Those same friends will only say this because they recognize you're in a bad marriage. Your friends and family likely see something that you apparently don't choose to see. This is because they are dispassionate witnesses. Love is blind so despite your chicks glaring problems, you will not want to see them. As was once famously quipped, love is:

> *"A temporary insanity curable by marriage"*
>
> *Ambrose Bierce*

What Mr. Bierce was attempting to recognize is that you can "love" someone all you want but marriage will make you reevaluate that love. Every man (and likely every woman) goes through the same cycle. Marriage is no joke and the decision to marry will leave you asking, "Why in the hell did I get married?".

Now, if you are going to disregard all these words of warning I'm imparting upon you, fine, that's totally your choice, but be prepared to be the best husband you can be. It will no doubt be hectic and there WILL be many times that you contemplate leaving or taking up a mistress. There may even be times where you contemplate faking your own death to achieve peace and freedom on a small island in the

Mediterranean[56]. There will definitely be those times where you contemplate homicide. Obviously, I implore you to disregard that last fantasy; you psycho bastard. You must do the best you can within the confines of your morality. Ask yourself the hard questions and determine if you are really ready for marriage. Ask yourself:

Can the woman you are thinking about marrying be your greatest long-term best-friend?

If you have not had any problems with this woman, nor seen any hard times in your burgeoning relationship, she is just a friend for the moment, you don't really know her. Step back and pretend you are advising your best friend if he were contemplating what you are about to do. There is no doubt, you would tell your buddy to give it a bit more time before he got married. Perhaps, you should think about your decision some more.

Your lady had better be someone who shares your same dreams, the same wishes, the same goals, and most importantly, similar hobbies, food tastes, sexual interests, and taste in TV shows because this is the stuff you will spend most of your time doing

---

[56] Most married men have seriously dreamed about this, although the polling data is at best, sketchy.

together (Yes including watching TV). If you both do not share the same or similar interests, you both better be willing to accept the others' quirks. **Opposites may attract, but those who are similar, are already compatible.**

To leave on a positive note, there are several benefits to marriage... *But, unfortunately, I can't think of any of them right now.* The bottom line is that nothing can prepare you for marriage but since you've read this book, you should be better equipped to handle the gunfight you're voluntarily getting ready to charge in to. So, if you ask me whether or not you should marry, I'd say absolutely not, but that won't matter since you won't listen to the many married guys you've already asked. You're still going to think you will be different than the rest of us.

No one wants to end up in a divorce but you have to accept that sometimes, it happens. It's nothing personal! It just **happens** occasionally. Marriages regularly wither and die away just as car engines and knees do. They get worn down and become useless. They become so painful that you (or your chick) may one day go crazy and be featured on the 10 O'Clock News because either you beat her up (while wearing a wife-beater) or she stabbed you after you came home from the corner bar in a drunken stupor.

If your girlfriend or wife is as crazy as you tell your friends she is, be careful. It was little more than a decade ago that Lorena Bobbitt chopped off her husbands "little guy" in that national case that seemingly lasted for years. Luckily the police were able to find his wiener in all its ant-covered glory, right where she threw it out of her moving car as she sped away into the darkness. John Bobbitt was able to get it sewn back on but maybe you won't be so lucky. Choose very wisely, and good luck with that! But please promise not to do a porn movie when you get yours sewn back on as Bobbitt[57] did. Yucky!

Banked Trust and Marriage Phases

There are four phases of marriage. They are the Newlywed, Settling, Depressing, and Divorcing Phases. These phases are all part of the **Banked Trust Average**. A nuclear power plant that is fueled by Plutonium 239 rods as fuel will generate electricity at its highest level just after rods are newly installed. The nuclear reactor will become less and less effective as the plutonium rods are used.   This is how marriage works, except you cannot replace the fuel.

To maintain a marriage, you must avoid the negative aspects of the marriage phases and try your best to prolong the positive aspects. Those who can figure out how to do so will maintain long marriages. It is valuable to understand that these phases elapse differently for everyone and Individual tendencies determine how much trust an individual requires.

---

[57] Bobbitt starred in two porno flicks after the incident; John Wayne Bobbit: *Uncut* (1994), and *Frankenpenis* (1996)..

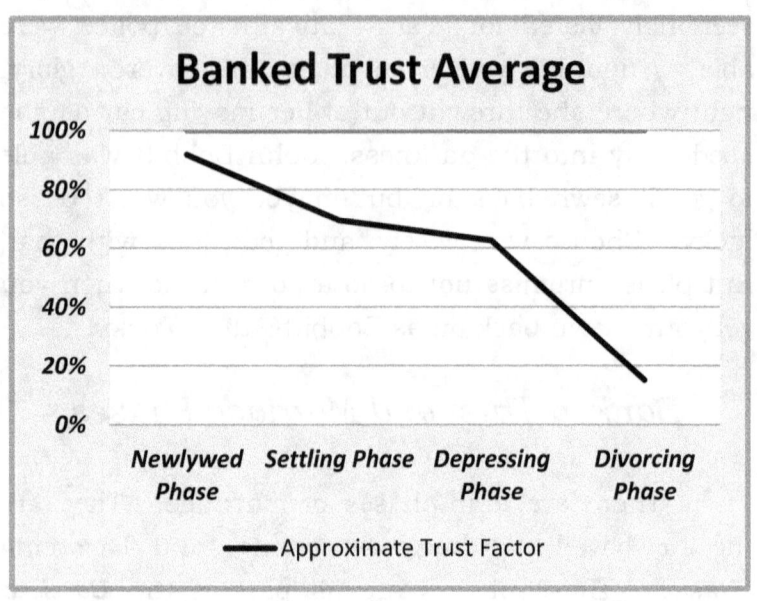

Banked Trust Average

Newlywed Phase · Settling Phase · Depressing Phase · Divorcing Phase

——Approximate Trust Factor

The **Newlywed Phase** occurs immediately after the courting (which is NOT a phase of marriage). Newlyweds are represented by their optimistic idealism of marriage and their willingness to take on the future as a couple. This is the phase that most unmarried people believe an entire marriage **is** like. Many young, and dumb people think that in a perfect world... it is POSSIBLE to have an entire marriage that is just like the typical newlywed phase. Nope! One year is the popularly recognized newlywed phase.

A **Settling Phase** begins when newlyweds move into the daily operations of life as a married couple. This begins when a couple realizes that marriages are hard. This is usually accompanied with stress in the realization that the newlywed phase is over. Kids may come about during this phase. This phase is generally, the longest lasting phase of marriage when spouses are working on their careers and generally finding their place as both individuals, and as a couple.

A **Depressing Phase** is a byproduct of the realization that they are, in fact, stuck in their marriage situation, whatever that may be. This phase can last for numerous years. The length of this phase is extended by settling phase factors to include financial realities, parenthood, and most importantly, familiarization with spouse. Common questions depressed spouses ask themselves are, "how can I get out of my mortgage?", or "am I too old to start over"? Generally, no action will be taken in this phase.

The **Divorcing Phase** is the final phase of a marriage. This phase doesn't so much begin as it, develops. Some would say the divorcing phase starts within the previous phases of marriage. When trust and communication within a marriage has been exhausted and one or both parties realize there will be no redress of their grievances. There may or may not be a separation because it is not always obvious to both spouses how catastrophic their situation has become. This phase is usually complete when one party has had enough and packs it up.

Although I've described Banked Trust and the Marriage Phases in the context of a couple, these phases also take place individually within each spouse. To have a successful marriage and deal with these phases, you'll have to accept and address the **_Law Of Diminished Respectability_** which states:

The longer you are married to someone, the more diminished your respect for them will become.

People obviously date and marry those whom they adore and respect greatly. While she is new and shiny, a man has the height of respect he will ever have for a woman. A man will never love a woman more than while he is dating her. Given enough time, boredom, and frustration, respect for each other will quickly melt away. Although there will be respect spikes such as when a husband gets a huge raise, or a wife has a baby, trending will ensure long-term respect will only decline over the course of a marriage.

It is always fascinating that despite any bad news or serious concerns, single people fail to listen to anyone with *actual* marriage experience. Bachelors will continue to think marriage is a reasonable idea. You, and millions like you, will attempt marriage because of the few that occasionally appear to succeed. We all hope that we'll be one of those success stories but the statistics say that if you're an American, you're about 50 percent likely to divorce.[58]

---

[58] The Future of Marriage in America," University of Virginia and the National Marriage Project, 2007

7

...And We Are Done Here

> *"When two people decide to get a divorce, it isn't a sign that they "don't understand" one another, but a sign that they have, at last, begun to."*
>
> *Helen Rowland*

Sadly, you've come to the end of our book. If you've paid attention, you've learned some lessons that may keep you safe and secure in your future. These are priceless truths that you should consider prior to marrying. Robert Half was quoted as saying: ***"Free advice... is worth the price"***, however, if you choose to disregard what I say in this book; you do so at your own peril.

You men, and the few ladies that have angrily made it to the end of this book, must recognize that you have a difficult decision to make. Men will have to decide whether or not to marry! Women will have to decide if they want to listen to what a married man recognizes is important in a peaceful marriage. Unfortunately, many of you will make your decision without accepting the complete information.

There Are No Systems!!!

I would like to say I had a system, but, alas, I do not. I've said it before and I'll say it again; ***There Are No Systems***! And if there were such a system to determine or otherwise predict successful marriages, the inventor would immediately become a billionaire and win a Nobel Peace Prize[59] because people would get married confident they married the right person.

You must base your decision to marry on your own ingenuity, experience, and not your expectations.

---

[59] ... not that a Nobel Prize means anything anymore since President Obama got one when he hadn't even done anything at that point.

Systems CAN NEVER WORK because systems cannot predict the inconsistencies between individuals and their individual realities. The problem is choice and each person makes their own choice based on what they "hope" to achieve, their knowledge, intellect, and experience. Hopes cannot be addressed or predicted by a dating service. Nor by your mother's church group -- who have decided they are 'gonna "fix you up" with that girl that has *the great personality*[60].

For The Ladies Only

OK Ladies. Now I'm sure that some of you have made it to the end of this book. I know you may think this is a terrible message to send out but I want to give you my compliments. Despite your being horrified that anyone would suggest that *men shouldn't get married* and being further dismayed by the radical concept that *divorces aren't always the fault of the man.* You have learned a bit of how men think about marriage.

Now, if you are a woman that thinks that this is total crap and has no validity or basis in truth, you have a huge problem and you may have missed the point of the book entirely. By reading this book, you are witness to what many men believe happens to girlfriends after marriage. Presumably, by being

---

[60] "Great Personality" is code for "hideous beast" .

familiar with the concerns and thinking process of a man, a woman will make a more reasonable wife.

If you have not learned anything, what will happen in your future is all too predictable. You will, treat your husband as an extension of yourself and end up in a divorce because you're not smart enough to figure out that you may not know all you **THINK** you know. Nor have you figured out that a husband (or any man) is not an extension of your dreams and desires. He is an individual with goals, dreams, and behaviors of his own. You should support each other and never stifle. If he wants to **try** to build an airplane, let him.

Now I'm fully aware that this book may make us dudes seem, well, shallow, but maybe you'll benefit and learn to appreciate us more because you'll have become aware of what your man will lose by marrying your crazy, conceited, selfish ass. No longer will you be able to treat your spouse like your father treated "his little girl", when you were a teeny-bopper chick with the heartthrob posters (no doubt some douche named "Corey") hanging on your bedroom walls right above your teddy bears.

Whatever you think about this book, just know that if you make these mistakes, you will never be happy and marriage will grow to suck both yours, and your husband's soul dry. You'll eventually give up and then blame your soon to be ex-husband for all of your anger. You may or may not play the victim but it won't matter one bit. You'll end up fat, sad, and angry that you lost the best years of your life.

You don't have to believe me, but you ignore me at your own peril. It may not sound pretty, but you know what? It's the truth... and sometimes the truth isn't pretty. At the end of the day, it's a toss-up. I hope you recognize that this book was worth reading and that you gain a better relationship with your man through understanding of what and how he thinks.

Men, Now You Have The Wisdom

Men must pay close attention, focus, and truly decide if marriage is for them, and this must be based on the information they learn about marriage. There will come a moment when many men believe they've found their possible future wife and must determine if this person is really, truly what they **NEED** and not merely what they **WANT**.. We all want hot chicks, but we need character. If you can figure out how to sort the two apart, let the rest of us know.

I know it will be uncomfortable because you may feel as though you're in "love", but logically, if you believe in "love", your infatuation cannot really be love because you barely know this girlie-girl. So, let's just assume that you are pussy-whipped, because you likely are. You have to sort some issues out because if you don't, they will lead you in to an uncomfortable, foreseeable, divorce. We have discussed several of these themes throughout the book, however, here is a wrap-up of concerns you should consider about your lady that will help quickly weed-out the ones that you don't stand a chance with.

- Is she going to nag you when she doesn't get what she wants from you?
- Is she going to TRY to stop you from hanging out with your friends after you get married?
- Is she going to work after you get married?
- Is she going to ask you to get rid of your car or stuff after you get married?
- Is she going to go back to work after she has a kid[61]? Two kids? Five kids?
- Are there any areas of sex she finds disgusting, disturbing, or repulsive... that you may want?
- Do you think your life will be improved because of your marriage to this lady?
- Do you want to have kids NOW?
- Are there any sexual acts that she wants to try someday that you might find offensive?[62]
- Are you prepared to go into massive debt buying your wife a bunch of useless crap you won't use?
- Will she sign a pre-nuptial agreement?

With the possible exception of the pre-nuptial agreement thing, I assure you that **all** of these other questions WILL come up in the course of your marriage. Discuss these areas with your girlfriend, fiancé, or perspective wife and hopefully (but not likely), she will be honest and give you all the

---

[61] She will say yes, but the answer will be a resounding no once that child hits her belly.

[62] ...yea right! I know but I had to put it out there. I know you're definitely not into those yucky threesomes.

information you need to make an informed decision. The most likely outcome is that she won't tell you the truth for fear you won't marry her ass. She'd rather start a relationship on lies. That's why she has so "underestimated" the number of dudes she's slept with. I know you didn't want to hear that from me but, now you know. Your future wife is a slut!!

Some of the other areas may seem far-fetched and you may even think they won't be an issue for you in the glorious marriage you are about to partake in... But just remember, if you're reading this book; You obviously don't know what the hell you're talking about! This is why you sought out wisdom and bought this book in the first place.

> *"The difference between a divorce and a legal separation is that a legal separation gives a husband time to hide his money."*
> *Johnny Carson*

Ask yourself a question. If this book is not realistic, then, reading this book won't hurt your situation at all. You lose nothing by merely broaching the subjects in this book with the lady you're thinking about getting *hitched* to. Hell, if you have to, turn this book into a big joke and act like you're not serious. Use it stir communication between you.

Men reading this hopefully have a better idea of what to expect from marriage. Some guys will learn something, some will not. Many others will fall for all of the traps and wind-up in a horrid marriage that will end in a tragic and fiery divorce, or a fratricide event[63]. This will happen all because they couldn't read a stupid – **but supremely incredible** – book for a few hours and contemplate the message for a few weeks!

> *"There are four stages in a marriage. First there's the affair, then the marriage, then children and finally the fourth stage, without which you cannot know a woman, the **divorce**."*
>
> *Norman Mailer*

What the vast majority of married guys merely want - as if it matters - is peace. We definitely don't want to deal with much of the bull-shit women reap upon us! If there is no peace, then the marriage can't work over the long-term. Women that continue to bring stress and drama will eventually find that their husband will do what he has to do to rid his environment of stressors. Left unchecked, or if a man cannot get away from the stress the woman foists upon him, he will eventually go for the divorce because it is less stressful than the marriage. Get it?

When you as the man do finally give up on marriage, you must understand that your first inclination will be to blame your wife for the divorce but just remember that you are not blameless. If you

---

[63] "Officer, It was an accident, I swear!"

just paid attention, you wouldn't have even got married. Instead of blaming her, accept that you are responsible for your poor selection and decision-making as well.

If you're lucky, you'll have avoided a costly marriage that forced you to miss out on the real "love" of your life. You will have avoided the loss of "stuff" that you've worked so very hard to collect to which some judge gave away to your *soon-to-be* ex-wife. This might include a great house, maybe a few beloved cars, and the random items you used to decorate your bachelor pad.

When all else fails; *for-the-love-of-all-that-is-good-and-holy*, limit the number of times you get married to two times. Realistically, if you divorce once, you can justify it by pointing at the faults of your ex, but with two divorces, everyone will know you must have some issues. With three divorces, you're most-likely crazy. Don't be a crazy, self-hating, bastard!

As for reasons to marry, the first marriage can be your experimentation at the concept of "love" (since you want to believe in it) and the second (or any afterward) should be limited to financial reasons. If a lady is rich and wants your fat, poor, balding ass as a paid manwhore (which would be utterly unthinkable), **go for it** knowing that love's got nothing to do with it and you just want money and travel out of it.

For a final bit of logic for you – dumber – gentlemen out there. Guys have been getting married for eons, or at least centuries, and the story has been the same for just as long. Guys are dissatisfied and the more we try to treat women as equals, the more problems we seem to have. Now I'm not suggesting we are anything but equals in life and value, but in marriage we are extremely different animals.

Guys think differently, and women look better. Guys are more random and aggressive, while women are more nurturing and reasonable. Guys build space shuttles and women build anger in guys. Don't fight it! Get used to it! Accept it! In relationships, guys and their wives have different roles. Men are men, and women will constantly attempt to change their men.

It is my contention that men will ALWAYS be dissatisfied with marriage, but not to worry. They will continue to marry because they won't listen to anyone. Hopefully, I helped a few misguided men to avoid the marriage delusion. They had better understand that if they choose to marry (despite all logic and good wisdom) they should do so merely because they want to.

Do yourself a favor and do not get married. Always remember that Wives Wreck Lives. So stay away!

Although there is admittedly some satire and perhaps even a bit of sarcasm involved in my presentation, I most definitely believe that everything in this book is based on fact. If you ask the majority of married men, they'll corroborate my concerns. So hate me if you will, but know that if you declare this all crap and don't entertain the thought and purpose behind it, you may miss an opportunity to build a tight relationship or repair a waning one. The hope is that you find a bit of happiness for yourself in the form of a stable mate. You **might** even build a stable marriage.

Now I've told you what I'm thinking and feeling about marriage. Educate and learn for yourself what marriage is [to you]. Make your own decision, but as I said in the beginning of the book, **it won't matter if you read this or not <u>because you are a man</u>** and you think you know everything already. No one can tell you a damn thing and if they did, you wouldn't believe them anyway.

Despite all of the marriage challenges you will overcome as a husband, you will still join the fraternity of men who will risk and likely lose half of their stuff to a hideous divorce. You can continue to dream that your story will somehow be different than every other guys marriage story throughout mankind and that's okay, but you have to recognize that you are NOT the first guy to fall into the marriage trap, and obviously, you won't be the last.

www.ingramcontent.com/pod-product-compliance
Lightning Source LLC
Chambersburg PA
CBHW072137280526
45788CB00002B/675